The Sock Knitter's Workshop

Everything Knitters Need to Knit Socks Beautifully

EWA JOSTES AND STEPHANIE VAN DER LINDEN

Watson-Guptill Publications
NEW YORK

CONTENTS

MATERIALS 5

Yarn 5
Care 6
Needles 7
Other Useful Items 9

BASICS AND TIPS 11

The Basics — Socks for Beginners 17

CASTING ON 19

Tips on Casting On 19
How Many Stitches to Cast On? 20
Thumb Cast-on Method 21
Tubular (or Italian) Cast-on Method 23
Two-Needle Cast-on Method 26
Loop Cast-on Method 27
Invisible Cast-on Method 27

CUFFS 29

Ribbed Cuffs 29
Ribbed Cuffs with a Tubular Cast-on 30
Garter Cuffs 31
Double Cuffs 32
Frilly Cuffs 33
Rolled Cuffs 34
The Leg 35

HEELS 37

Fitting the Heel 37
Tips on Working the Heel 38

HEELS WITH HEEL FLAPS 40
Tips on Working a Heel Flap 41
Turning a Heel over 3 Panels 43
Turning a Horseshoe Heel over 4 Panels 45
Turning a Heart-Shaped Heel over 2 Panels 48
Round Heel 49

HEELS WITH DIAGONAL SEAMS 52
Short-Row Heel 53
Short-Row Heel with Reinforced Double Stitches ... 56
Short-Row Heel with Round Shaping 57
Wrap Stitch Heel 58
Gusset with Increases and Decreases 60
Hybrid Heel 61
Mock Short-Row Heel 63

ROUND HEELS JOINED AT THE FOOT 64
Tips on Working Round Heels 64
Plain Heel 66
Peasant Heel 67
"Afterthought" Heel with a Waste Yarn 69

TOES 71

Paired-Decrease Toes 71
Anatomically Shaped Toes 73
Star Toes 73
Spiral Toes 75
Flower Toes 76
Diagonal Seam Heel for Toes 77
Propeller Toes 78

OTHER SOCK KNITTING TECHNIQUES 81

Toe-Up Socks — Starting at the Toes 81
Toe-Up Toes 82
Heels for Toe-Up Socks 87
Finishes for Toe-Up Socks 90

SOCKS KNIT WITH CIRCULAR NEEDLES 93
Knitting with Two Circular Needles 93
Knitting with One Circular Needle in Rounds ... 95
Knitting Flat (Back and Forth)
    with One Circular Needle 97

PATTERNS 98

Baby's Socks 99
Garter Waves 100
Entirely Natural 101
Chevron Socks 102
For the Well-Respected Man 103
A Timeless Classic 104
For Mother and Daughter 105
Wavy Stripes 107
Anatomical Socks 108
Ribs and Cables 109
Sport Socks 110
Socks for Shopping 111
Mosaic Pattern 112
Folklore Socks 113
Basket Weave Socks 114

TRANSFERRING PATTERNS 116

YARN SUBSTITUTION CHARTS 119

SIZE CHARTS 120

RESOURCES 126

INDEX 127

ABOUT THE AUTHORS 128

Handknitting socks today is as popular as ever. Everyone adores those cuddly masterpieces. They radiate their own unique "personality" that simply can't be achieved by machine. It's almost as if some of the time and love that's invested in them as they're being made is actually knitted in. They simply are something really special.

Over hundreds of years this knowledge was passed on from needle to needle, because knitting socks was an absolute necessity. Techniques for handknitting socks weren't entirely lost following the introduction of machine-knit socks, but only the basics were passed on, if at all. With just one or two heel designs, or only one method for toe shaping that might not be to the intended wearer's liking, there were few options for making a sock that really fit well, so it's hardly surprising that people were disappointed with the results. Gradually, this valuable knowledge nearly vanished because no one considered it necessary to pass on those remaining techniques to the next generation.

Today we find that young women in particular want to learn how to knit socks; frequently their mothers either don't remember how or never learned. *The Sock Knitter's Workshop* not only aims to address that lack of knowledge by demonstrating the process clearly and concisely, it's also a comprehensive and practical collection of clearly explained lessons, accompanied by step-by-step photographs and diagrams, that enables anyone—even someone who's new sock knitting—to quickly complete her very first pair.

For more experienced knitters, this book provides a complete overview, with new ideas, new things to try, and ways of optimizing a sock's fit, making it a great reference book, as well as a sourcebook of elements for creating your own sock designs. We've collected different ways of casting on, and of working the cuff, heels, and toes gathered from different traditions, according to knitting technique and the final result. We've also included several patterns at the end of the book that combine a variety of techniques. Discover the fun of playing with the individual elements. The possibilities are virtually endless. Enjoy!

Stephanie van der Linden

and *Ewa Jostes*

MATERIALS

What do you need to knit socks? Well, really just yarn and needles! But before you get started, it's worthwhile to read about these materials and tools.

Yarns

FIBER AND PLIES

New wool is the classic sock yarn. But rubbing causes wool to pill (form the dreaded balls and fluff). This doesn't just look bad, but in time it also causes the fabric to get thinner and thinner. In order to prevent rapid abrasion in shoes, it's advisable to use a wool blend that includes about 20 to 30% nylon (also known as polyamide). Today's sock yarns usually undergo special treatment so that they are washable at 104°F/40°C, do not felt, and may even be suitable for tumble drying. Sock yarns are available in a range of thicknesses.

The most popular sock yarn used is fingering weight, sometimes referred to as 4-ply. Socks made from this are warmer and thicker than machine-made ones but thin enough to wear in ordinary shoes.

For thick socks that are made to be worn with boots in winter, or as slipper socks, use DK or sport-weight, or 6-ply sock yarn. But since socks made with coarser yarns can be uncomfortable on the foot, 6-ply yarn can only be used up to a point.

Particularly complicated sock patterns with a lot of stitches, such as those adorned with cables, are frequently worked in baby-weight or 3-ply sock yarn.

Because lace-weight or 2-ply sock yarn is so incredibly thin, it isn't suitable for sock knitting. But it is ideal for darning, as a waste yarn, or for reinforcement; and it is frequently available in the same colors as baby, fingering, and DK or sport sock yarns in small skeins.

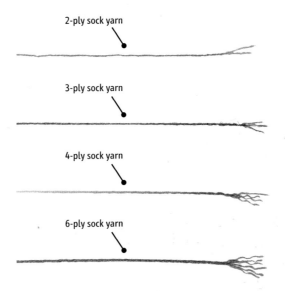

2-ply sock yarn

3-ply sock yarn

4-ply sock yarn

6-ply sock yarn

Although ply is not necessarily linked to weight, sock yarns referred to by the number of their plies often correspond to the yarn weights in the chart below.

SOCK YARNS AND THEIR USES

	CYC Standard (see chart on page 119)	Skein Length 3½ oz./100g	Gauge 4 x 4" (10 x 10cm)	Needle size (also in mm)	Yarn Quantity (for one pair up to men's size 14 in stockinette stitch)	Yarn Usage
Lace (2-ply)	Approx. No. 1	897 yd./820m				sock and waste yarn
Baby (3-ply)	Approx. No. 1 or 2	570 yd./520m	32 stitches x 46 rows	0–2/1.5–2.75	2½ oz./70g	for complicated patterns with lots of stitches
Fingering (4-ply)	Approx. No. 1	460 yd./420m	30 stitches x 42 rows	1–3/2.0–3.0	3½ oz./100g	general sock size, for all patterns and stockinette stitch
DK or Sport (6-ply)	Approx. No. 2 or 3	275 yd./250m	22 stitches x 30 rows	3–7/3.25–4.5	5¼ oz./150g	for warm socks in stockinette stitch, patterns are bulky

BLENDS

Blends made up of various materials give each yarn its particular qualities.

Cotton sock yarn (for example, 40% new wool, 35% cotton, and 25% nylon) is very popular for summer socks. The added cotton ensures that it doesn't get as warm as classic sock yarn. Amazingly, many people who are allergic to wool or who suffer from dermatitis have no reaction to this yarn, despite the new wool. Since the cotton yarn lies firmer in your hand, it is very easy to try to knit this looser or with larger/fatter needles. But this would lead to the stitches becoming soft and shapeless after the first wash. Cotton yarn is frequently offered in less bold colors or blended with lighter shades since cotton doesn't absorb dye as well as new wool. Since strongly dyed cotton sock yarns require more fixing agent for the dyes and other additives, it might be preferable to use pastel shades.

Silk sock yarn (for example, 55% new wool, 25% nylon, and 20% silk) has an elegant sheen and really brings out the details of the patterns. The yarn is very soft and cool to the skin, and, like cotton sock yarn, shouldn't be knit up too loosely. Silk yarns are available in beautiful, bold colors and are also machine washable; but because dyed silk often runs for the first couple of washes, socks knitted with it should be washed separately.

Bamboo sock yarn (for example, 45% bamboo fiber, 40% new wool, and 15% nylon) has only been available for a few years. It's very smooth and even softer than sock yarn made with silk. Bamboo yarn should also not be knitted up too loosely. It slips very easily on metal needles, so that experienced knitters frequently have difficulty keeping their stitches under control.

Stretch sock yarn (for example, 70% new wool, 25% nylon, and 5% polyester) contains a small proportion of elastic that gives socks more stretch. It's tempting to knit these yarns a little tightly, but since this would undermine the stretch effect, it's best to knit them on larger needles.

Yarn manufacturers have been producing lots of new blends over the past years. They concentrate mainly on natural alternatives for the nylon blends with similar qualities, since many knitters prefer purely natural yarns. There are bound to be many new developments in this field over the next few years. Natural yarns consisting of 75% new wool and 25% bamboo fiber; of 60% new wool, 20% bamboo fiber, and 20% silk; or of 85% new wool and 15% ramie are already on the market and becoming increasingly popular.

Care

Before buying the yarn, take a sniff of each ball. The more the yarn smells of wool, the less it has dried out. Before being processed, new wool has most of its lanolin removed so it will absorb the dyes and fixing agents better. The drier (or more fat-free) the wool is, the scratchier it feels to the skin. The cure for this is a one-time application of lanolin, which is sold in drugstores. Such a treatment usually lasts for one or two years even if the socks are machine washed using ordinary detergents. Another cause of scratchy wool is too many suds in the woolen fibers. If some of the detergent remains in the wool, the socks will feel hard and rough. Add a dash of white vinegar to the last rinse in the machine to make the socks soft and fluffy again. One to two tablespoons of vinegar are enough for a machine load of washing. This won't have any effect on the other items in the load, as vinegar has a naturally antibacterial effect; and by adding so little, the smell will disappear quickly after the cycle is completed.

Needles

Needles come in all sorts of thicknesses, lengths, materials, and variations. Here's a quick overview of the various types of needles to use to get the best sock-knitting results.

DOUBLE-POINTED NEEDLES

Double-pointed needles usually come as a set of five needles of the same length and thickness, with points at each end. In order to work in rounds, the stitches are distributed evenly across four needles. The free, fifth, needle is the working needle that you use to knit the stitches off the others. When you've worked all stitches off one needle, the newly empty needle now becomes the working needle.

Double-pointed needles used for knitting socks are usually about 8"/20cm long, though shorter needles that are just 6"/15cm long are also used. Some manufacturers offer "between" sizes as well.

Double-pointed needles made of nickel-coated steel are very smooth and hard. The stitches slide very well, with hardly any resistance, and the needles feel cool to the touch. Since steel needles are a little heavier, they're more suited to fine knitwear made with thinner needles; and because they're so hard, even thin ones hardly bend and it's

virtually impossible to break them. They're available from size 0/1.25mm. People with nickel allergies or who suffer from rheumatism are advised not to use these needles.

Double-pointed needles made of powder-coated aluminum are a perfect alternative. These metal needles are considerably lighter, if not quite as smooth. They provide good support for the knitting but bend easily in your hands. However, it is very easy to bend them back into shape again. These needles are available from size 1/2.0mm.

Double-pointed needles made of bamboo are warm to the touch and bend considerably more than metal needles, which some people find rather annoying. Bamboo needles should be made from harder varieties such as winter bamboo; otherwise, the tips of the needles will fray and become unusable. If you knit too tightly, you risk breaking the needle. Bamboo needles are available from size 1/2.0mm.

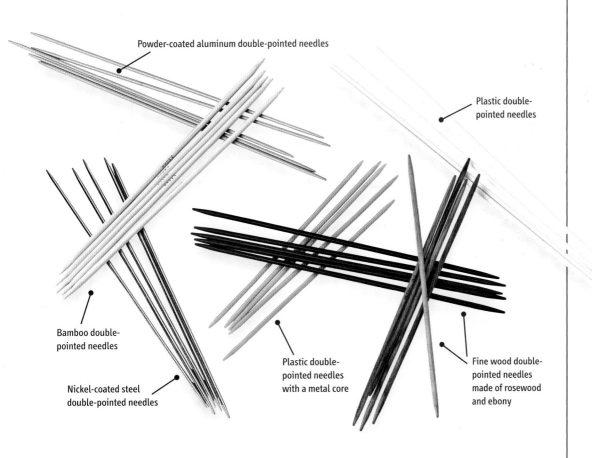

Powder-coated aluminum double-pointed needles

Plastic double-pointed needles

Bamboo double-pointed needles

Nickel-coated steel double-pointed needles

Plastic double-pointed needles with a metal core

Fine wood double-pointed needles made of rosewood and ebony

Keep your fine wood needles in good condition by wiping them with a little linseed oil from time to time. Any rough spots can quickly be eliminated with a piece of fine-grade sandpaper.

Double-pointed needles made of fine wood such as rosewood, ebony, or beech are a real treat for your hands. (They're frequently made from the leftover scraps of wood used to build musical instruments.) They have an even smoothness and feel warm to the touch. Because they'll entice you to knit more loosely, make sure you pay special attention to your gauge swatch when using them. Unfortunately, these needles can break if treated too harshly, so treat them gently. Wooden needles are usually available from size 2/2.75mm. Double-pointed needles are also made from birch, which is slightly harder; and the shorter length of 5"/12.5cm is available from size 1/2.0mm.

Plastic double-pointed needles are made mainly in the larger sizes—from about 8 to 17/5.0 to 12.0mm—because metal needles get too heavy and wooden needles are too expensive. Some of the thin plastic needles are also stabilized with a metal core. In more recent years the market has seen needles made from Galalith, a natural form of plastic. This artificial material is a little harder than plain plastic but yet is very flexible. Double-pointed needles made from this are already available from size 3/3.0mm. However, heat, cold, and low humidity can affect the plastic over time, causing it to crack, so these needles should be treated with care.

CIRCULAR NEEDLES

Circular needles are best described as two same-size needles joined together by a flexible length of plastic. This way you have the same advantage as you do with double-pointed needles: you can work from both ends of the needles. This advantage can be put to use especially when knitting socks with two circular needles (see page 93).

Circular needles come in many different sizes and lengths. Socks are usually knit using circular needles in sizes 1 to 5/2.0 to 3.75mm and are available in lengths of 24 to 32"/60 to 80cm. Circular needles are usually made from nickel-coated steel or powder-coated aluminum. Circular needles made from bamboo or fine woods start at size 2/2.75mm.

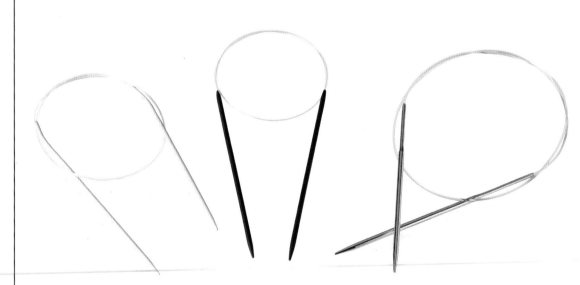

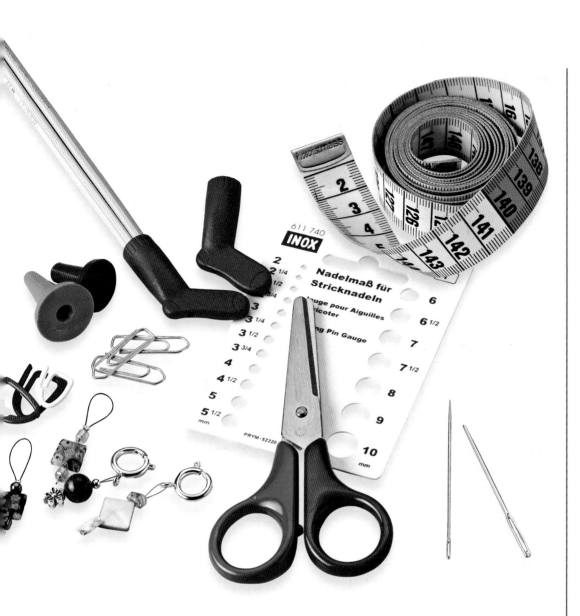

Other Useful Items

Use a blunt tapestry, embroidery, or darning needle to pull the last stitches together without the risk of inserting the needle into the yarn. If, however, the needle is to go through the yarn—for instance, to weave in the yarn tails—then a sharp-pointed tapestry, embroidery, or darning needle is much better. A cable needle is used to hold stitches to the side until required. Scissors cut the yarn evenly, and a tape measure or ruler allows you to measure the length of the foot accurately. If you have a large number of double-pointed needles in differing sizes, you'll also appreciate a needle gauge, which is a piece of plastic into which holes with a precise diameter have been cut. Insert needles into these holes to quickly and easily determine their size.

There are other knitting aids that are generally not needed for knitting socks. What's more important is somewhere comfortable to sit, good lighting, and a pleasant atmosphere. Granddad's old cigar box can become a real treasure box for your needles and other knitting supplies, and a basket or a lockable box can hold your knitting. Plastic stitch markers can be replaced by paper clips or by small homemade stitch markers with pretty bead dangles.

BASICS
AND TIPS

If you've never knit a sock before, it's helpful to think of it as a closed tube with a kink for the heel. Socks should be without seams or lumps and bumps, which would make wearing them very uncomfortable. This is why they're usually knit seamlessly, in rounds. In contrast to sweaters knit in the round, the circumference of each sock is so small that you need to work with double-pointed needles in order to move freely when knitting. For that reason, the stitches are normally distributed evenly across four needles and knit with the fifth needle.

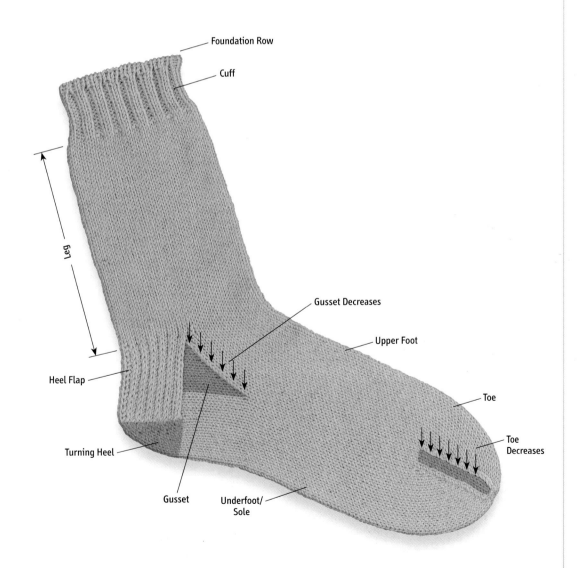

Foundation Row

Cuff

Leg

Gusset Decreases

Upper Foot

Heel Flap

Toe

Turning Heel

Toe
Decreases

Gusset

Underfoot/
Sole

Note

When closing the round, be careful not to twist the stitches!

NUMBERING DOUBLE-POINTED NEEDLES

To keep track of the sequence of your knitting, the needles are numbered from 1 to 4, starting with the point of the cast-on and then going in the direction in which you are working.

    To knit in rounds, the stitches of the foundation row are arranged evenly over four needles. The fifth, free needle is then used to knit one-quarter of the newly cast-on stitches. This arrangement of needles is called a 4 + 1 needle arrangement. (Knitters in some countries traditionally work with 3 + 1 needles instead of 4 + 1.) It's also possible to work with an arrangement of 1 or 2 circular needles (see page 93, "Knitting with Two Circular Needles").

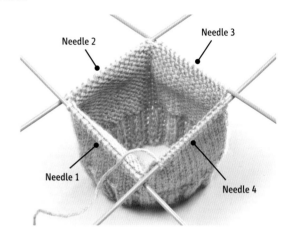

THE "CORRECT" NEEDLE SIZE

Everyone has his or her own way of holding the yarn when knitting and pulling the stitches tight. If you work the knitting too loosely, the finished socks will be too loose, causing the cuffs to stretch and the socks to slip down into the shoes, all of which will distort the stitch design. On the other hand, if you knit too tightly, the socks lose their elasticity, feel stiff, and might even pinch. Only the correct needle size can help alleviate these problems.

    The yarn label usually recommends several needle sizes; the smallest is for all those who knit relatively loosely,

while the largest is for those who knit more tightly. Depending on how you work, it might help to change needle sizes. The yarn label usually also indicates how many rows and stitches are needed to make a 4 x 4"/10 x 10cm gauge swatch in stockinette stitch in order to get the correct elasticity, because that's what makes a sock fit well. So if you want to knit using a different yarn, make sure you use the right-size needle to get the correct gauge, which can be confirmed only by knitting a gauge swatch.

KNITTING A GAUGE SWATCH

To make sure you are using the correct needle size, work a flat gauge swatch measuring about 4 x 4"/10 x 10cm in stockinette stitch in open rows. The foundation row, selvage stitches, and bound-off edge should not be included in your measurements.

    When using fingering-weight or 4-ply sock yarn, make a gauge swatch of 38 stitches and 50 rows; for DK-weight or

6-ply yarn, 28 stitches and 38 rows are enough. When the swatch is complete, carefully block it to the correct measurements: cover the swatch with a damp cloth or steam it carefully, and let it dry. If there are more stitches for every 4"/10cm than are indicated on the yarn label, use larger needles; if there are fewer stitches, use smaller needles.

UNWINDING YARN FROM THE INSIDE OF THE BALL OR SKEIN

Knitting is so much easier if you take the yarn from the inside of the ball, because then the ball will stay in one place as the yarn is unwound.

    When trying to find the end of the yarn inside the ball, you may pull out an entire piece; but don't worry—this extra length will knit up quickly in the first few rounds.

STARTING WITH THE SAME MOTIF ON SELF-PATTERNING YARNS

Many self-patterning yarns have repeating motifs or stripes. But beware: the balls don't all start with the same pattern sequence. If you want a pair of matching socks, you'll need to find a part of the yarn that's identical to the same pattern in the other ball before starting to cast on. This is something to keep in mind when working with obvious changes in stripes and patterns.

Tip

If you're working with two 1³/₄-oz./50g balls and have two sets of double-pointed needles to work with, you can select the appropriate color motif in each ball before starting to work, then cast on for both socks and possibly even work the cuffs. Then put one sock aside and complete the other sock first.

AVOIDING HOLES WHEN WORKING KNITWISE

If you're knitting in rounds for the first time, you'll notice that stitches between the needles can become rather wide. If these wide stitches are right above each other in all the rounds, the gaps will form a ladder in the finished socks. These holes occur because the yarn has to be pulled a little tighter when changing from one needle to another, which isn't the case when you are working with just one needle.

In order to get the feel of the correct tension needed, it's advisable when knitting in rounds for the first time to distribute the somewhat larger stitches on each needle evenly across the motif by moving the working needle by a few stitches each time. This is done by leaving the newly empty needle on one side after working the stitches, then working another 2 to 4 stitches with the needle used last before con-

tinuing with the working needle as usual. To keep track of the round change, always put in a stitch marker. Simply place a stitch marker (or a paper clip) after the last stitch on Needle 1 before knitting or purling it together with the first stitch on Needle 4 and work another 2 to 4 stitches from Needle 1. When you reach the marked position on the following rounds, just slip the marker from the left- to the right-hand needle and continue knitting. This way the round change will remain visible between Needles 4 and 1. When you reach the point where the heel has to be turned, simply rearrange the needles so they are in their original positions.

Example

A K2, P2 rib for the cuff after the foundation row based on 60 stitches can easily be arranged as 16 + 16 + 16 + 12 stitches to avoid holes. When changing to the leg pattern, rearrange the stitches so that there are 15 stitches on each needle.

Note

Knitwise = behind the
 left-hand stitch
Purlwise = behind the
 right-hand stitch

AVOIDING HOLES WHEN WORKING PURLWISE

The same problem with holes arises when you work stitches purlwise, such as when working knit and purl rib stitches for the cuff. Because the needle is held differently when working purlwise, this also changes the tension. You can overcome this problem by rearranging the stitches for the heel so that only the first stitch on each needle is a knit stitch.

RIGHT- AND LEFT-SLANTING DECREASES KNITWISE

When 2 stitches are worked together knitwise, the stitches slant to the right or left. If these decreases are worked over several rows or rounds in the same positions, this will create lines slanting to the left or right. This gives many heels and toes their characteristic appearance.

Knit Stitches

The most common way of working knit stitches is to insert the right-hand needle into the first stitch on the left-hand needle from left to right. Hold the working yarn behind the left-hand needle, carry it between the two needles toward the back of the work, then pull the yarn through the stitch on the left-hand needle with the tip of the right-hand needle and slip it off the left-hand needle.

Right- and left-slanting of knitwise decreases

Making a knit stitch:

Insert the right-hand needle into the stitch from left to right.

Carry the yarn between the two needles toward the back of the work.

Pull the loop through the stitch and slip it off the left-hand needle.

To make a **right-slanted decrease,** insert the needle through 2 stitches as if they were 1 stitch and knit both stitches together.

To make a **left-slanted decrease,** slip 2 stitches one after the other knitwise, then insert the left-hand needle from the front from left to right through both stitches and knit both

stitches off together. Left-slanting decreases that are made by working a slip decrease or are worked through the back of the loops create steps and uneven stitch sizes along the decreases that look unattractive.

Slip the first stitch from the left-hand to the right-hand needle.

Repeat for the second stitch.

Insert the left-hand needle through both slipped stitches.

Knit both stitches together knitwise.

In the following designs, the right-slanting decrease is described as knitting 2 stitches together knitwise. For the left-slanting decrease, we slip 2 stitches and knit the stitches together knitwise. Knitters who use the Eastern

method of knitting, in which the yarn is wound around the needle in the opposite direction, will have to work the other way; otherwise, for a right-slanting decrease, the stitches will slant to the left.

GRAFTING, OR KITCHENER STITCH

When grafting, also known as Kitchener stitch, you are joining two knitted panels with a seam that looks exactly like a row of knitting. Using a blunt embroidery needle, pick up and work the stitches of both panels, forming a new row of stitches. Each stitch has to be sewn twice. If you are brave enough to leave the last row of stitches open, you can work them following the instructions below.

Grafting is worked the same as duplicate stitch, which is used to embroider knitted panels.

Leaving unworked stitches of toes and heels open is very risky. The curvature causes the side stitches to be under tension, threatening to open them up quicker. Once this has happened, it is more difficult to pick up the stitches and also to try to repair dropped stitches for several rows or rounds.

It is much better and more practical to leave the last stitches on two parallel needles and to bind them off in a way that looks like actual knitting. To do this, cut the yarn long enough—usually about 20"/50cm is sufficient—and thread it onto a blunt embroidery needle.

Grafting open stitches

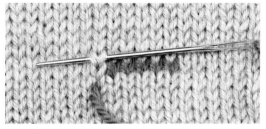

Duplicate stitch

Note

The best way to graft stitches is to lay the knit piece flat on a table. This way each stitch keeps its shape and can help prevent dropped stitches.

Preparing the first stitch:

Pick up the first of the front stitches purlwise, leaving the stitch on the needle.

Pick up the first of the back stitches knitwise, leaving the stitch on the needle.

Now bind off the stitches as for duplicate stitch:

Step 1:
Insert the needle knitwise into the stitch on the front needle, then lift the stitch (= right off).

Step 2:
Insert the needle purlwise into the stitch on the front needle, leaving the stitch on the needle (= left).

Step 3:
Insert the needle purlwise into the stitch on the back needle, then lift the stitch (= left off).

Step 4:
Insert the needle knitwise into the stitch on the back needle, leaving the stitch on the needle (= right).

Pull the yarn a little after every step. Always hold the working yarn below and to the right of the knitting needles. Repeat steps 1 to 4 until all the stitches are off the needles. Work the last 2 stitches as you normally would.

The mantra for grafting or working duplicate stitch is:
right off, left front; **left off, right** back.

Note

Needle holders for double-pointed needles, available in yarn and crafts stores, can be fitted to each end of all five double-pointed needles at the same time to hold all the needles together.

TRANSPORTING DOUBLE-POINTED NEEDLES

To prepare your knitting for transport, or to store it in a way that will avoid having it unravel, first wrap the working yarn firmly around one end and then around the other end, then around each end in a figure eight, thus holding the double-pointed needles and the empty needle firmly together. Two thin hair elastics will serve the same function.

Preparing double-pointed needles for transport

JOINING YARN THE RUSSIAN WAY

If you come across a knot in a strand of yarn, ideally you should cut it out and continue knitting as if you're picking up a new ball. When working with leftovers of a very special yarn, the question of how to make the transition neatly also arises. The easiest solution is to allow the ends of both yarns to hang down for about 6–8"/15–20cm at the back of the work and then to weave these in at the end. However, frequently the seam isn't as even as the remaining stitches, and the join is visible.

A more elegant solution is the Russian way. Thread the yarn tail onto a tapestry needle and twist it several times about 2"/5cm from the end of the needle so that it forms a loop. Thread the new yarn through this loop, thread the yarn through the tapestry needle too, and twist this again about 2"/5cm away through the thread of the new yarn. Pull both ends up firmly and cut any excess ends. Continue knitting with this newly attached yarn.

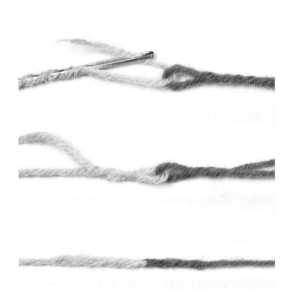

Joining yarn the Russian way

WEAVING IN YARN TAILS

To weave in all yarn tails firmly but without losing the fabric's visual continuity and elasticity, it's best to work the tails into the fabric on the diagonal.

To make sure that the stitches look even when you've finished knitting and weaving in the yarn tails, cover the completed sock with a damp cloth and let it dry, or steam it carefully, block lightly, and let it dry.

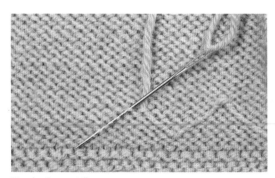

Weaving in yarn tails

And now you're ready to go! If you've already made socks before, you'll probably want to go straight to the chapters on each part of the sock—cuff, heel, and toe—which describe how to knit each part in detail and provide many variations. Any of these variations can be combined to suit your preference. Even experienced sock knitters will find something they haven't tried before.

The Basics—Socks for Beginners

Now knit your first sock!

For those of you who want step-by-step instructions for knitting a sock, just follow the red yarn to guaranteed success. Simply choose one of the two basic designs below and follow either the blue or red yarn through the book, which will guide you to the next design element. Both designs are easy to follow, even for beginners with limited knitting experience. It's advisable that you knit these socks using the recommended sock yarn, though either fingering (4-ply) or DK (6-ply) will work. The designs featured here were made from 3¹/₂ oz./100g Regia Cotton, Top Moda (4075) on size 2/2.75mm double-pointed needles.

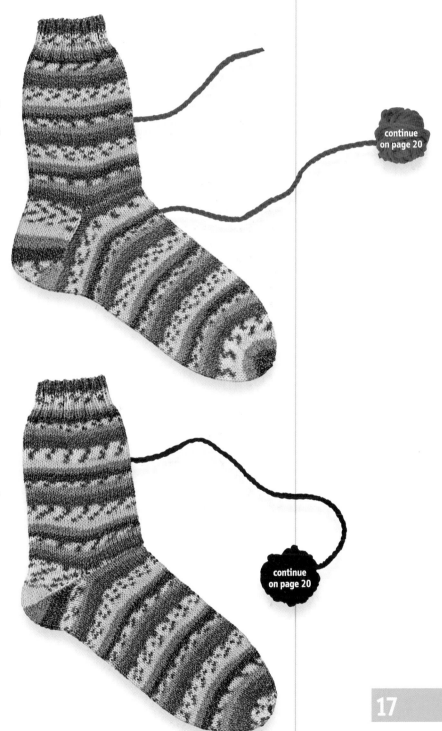

BASIC DESIGN 1
Classic with Heel Flap

The most basic heel design is the flap. To make the process of knitting this design and the first heel flap even easier, the sock is made with a heel flap consisting of just two sections instead of the usual three. As an example of classic heel flap sock designs, Basic Design 1 is a comfortable sock with lots of room across the arch.

If you opt for the comfortable Basic Design 1, follow the blue yarn through the book to find the instructions you'll need to knit it.

Basic Design 1 consists of the following sections:

- making a slip knot
- German thumb cast-on method
- 2 x 2 rib cuff
- leg
- heart-shaped heel
- foot
- paired decreases
- pulling stitches together
- weaving in yarn tails

continue on page 20

BASIC DESIGN 2
The Boomerang Heel

Basic Design 2 takes its name from the so-called boomerang heel. This is a heel with short rows, and it belongs to the family of diagonal seam heels. This is a popular alternative to the heel flap. The boomerang heel fits comfortably and is good to wear in shoes.

If you prefer to make Basic Design 2, follow the red yarn through the book to find the instructions you'll need to knit it.

Basic Design 2 consists of the following sections:

- making a slip knot
- German thumb cast-on method
- 2 x 2 rib cuff
- leg
- boomerang heel
- foot
- star toes
- pulling stitches together
- weaving in yarn tails

continue on page 20

CASTING ON

Before you can start knitting, you need to cast on. For socks, you need a cast-on that gives you enough stretch around the leg so that the sock doesn't cut in yet provides a smooth transition to the cuff, because the cuff has to keep its shape when worn.

Tips for Casting On

When closing the foundation row to form a round, make sure that the knitting does not twist, otherwise you have made a Moebius strip, which is of no use for making socks.

CASTING ON TO FOUR NEEDLES

Normally, stitches are cast on evenly across four double-pointed needles.

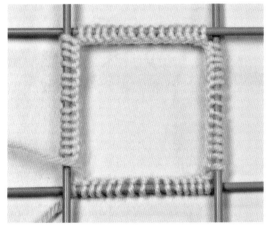 

Casting on to four needles, joining to form a ring on the first round

In comparison: cast on to a single needle on the first round and arrange the stitches evenly across four needles, joining to form a ring after the first row.

CASTING ON TO ONE NEEDLE

Joining to a round is much easier if you cast on all the stitches on one needle first.

After casting on all the stitches on just one needle, turn and work the stitches in a rib pattern, working one-quarter of the stitches on each double-pointed needle. Now it is easier to join to a round because the foundation edge is easier to recognize and pick up. The small gap between the first two rows can quickly and easily be closed when weaving in the yarn tail at the end of the work.

Beginners in particular tend to work the foundation row too tightly. To make sure that the foundation row is loose, use a larger needle—or alternately, work with two needles when casting on. Then to knit from the foundation row, carefully remove one of the two needles.

Cast on to two needles so that foundation row isn't too tight.

Tip

When joining to a round, avoid making the transition too loose by working the first 2 stitches from Needle 1 onto Needle 4 for a few rounds. Later, slip these 2 stitches back onto Needle 1 so that all the needles have the same number of stitches again.

continue
on page 21

continue
on page 21

MAKING A SLIP KNOT

To make this loop, which is often used to start a cast-on, hold a needle and the working yarn (the yarn that is coming from the ball) with your right hand and the hold the yarn tail with the middle finger, ring finger, and pinkie finger of your left hand. Now bring the yarn with your right hand once around your stretched-out thumb clockwise and then bring it down so that it forms a loop around your thumb. The working yarn and the yarn tail have now crossed in front of your thumb. Insert the needle into this loop from below and lift it off your thumb. Pull up the yarn with your left hand. The type of cast-on determines the length of the yarn tail.

Slip knot, crossing at thumb

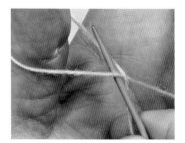
Insert the needle from below.

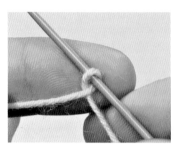
Completed slip knot

How Many Stitches to Cast On?

The number of stitches you need to cast on so that the sock fits properly depends on the circumference of the foot and the thickness of the yarn used. This does not mean that the foot has to be measured correctly. If you cast on according to your shoe size, you should find that the socks stretch enough to take into account for the different widths of feet. Only if you have very wide feet or ankles should you probably cast on according to the next shoe size up. The thicker the sock yarn is, the fewer the number of stitches that will be required. If you are using the usual fingering (4-ply) or

DK (6-ply) sock yarn, you can use the number of stitches given in the chart below. If you prefer to use other yarn, take the circumference of the sock in the respective size from the chart and calculate the number of stitches required using the gauge given on the yarn label. However, it is important to note that the thickness of the yarn must be included and taken into account. The thicker the yarn, the thicker the sock, and therefore the larger the circumference. For thick yarns, you should add $1/4$ to $1/2$"/0.5 to 1.5cm.

NUMBER OF STITCHES WITH FINGERING/4-PLY SOCK YARN (SEE PG. 119 FOR YARN EQUIVALENTS)
Length = $1^3/4$ oz./50g, 230 yards/210m, 30 stitches x 42 rows = 4 x 4"/10 x 10cm

Children's and women's sizes	5/5½	6/7	8/9	9½/10	11/11½	12/13	1/2	3/4	5/6	7/8	9/9½	10/11	12/13	14/15
Men's sizes										5/6	7/8	9/10	11/12	13/14
Continental sizes	20/21	22/23	24/25	26/27	28/29	30/31	32/33	34/35	36/37	38/39	40/41	42/43	44/45	46/47
Circumference	5¾"	5¾"	6¼"	6¼"	6¾"	6¾"	7¼"	7¼"	8"	8"	8¼"	8¼"	8¾"	9½"
Total stitches/ per needle	44/11	44/11	48/12	48/12	52/13	52/13	56/14	56/14	60/15	60/15	64/16	64/15	68/17	72/18

NUMBER OF STITCHES WITH DK/6-PLY SOCK YARN (SEE PG. 119 FOR YARN EQUIVALENTS)
Length = $1^3/4$ oz./50g, 137 yards/125m, 22 stitches x 30 rows = 4 x 4"/10 x 10cm

Children's and Women's sizes	5/5½	6/7	8/9	9½/10	11/11½	12/13	1/2	3/4	5/6	7/8	9/9½	10/11	12/13	14/15
Men's sizes										5/6	7/8	9/10	11/12	13/14
Continental sizes	20/21	22/23	24/25	26/27	28/29	30/31	32/33	34/35	36/37	38/39	40/41	42/43	44/45	46/47
Circumference	5¾"	5¾"	6½"	6½"	7"	7"	8"	8"	8½"	8½"	9"	9"	9"	10"
Total stitches/ per needle	32/8	32/8	36/9	36/9	40/10	40/10	44/11	44/11	48/12	48/12	52/13	52/13	52/13	56/14

Thumb Cast-on Method

This is one of the most common methods of casting on. It is easy to learn, quick to work, and forms a firm but stretchy edge. The stitches on both front and back look very neat.

The slip knot is worked with a single length of yarn that is at least three times as long as the circumference of the sock. Hold the needle with the slip knot in your right hand, the working yarn (the yarn that comes from the ball) over your outstretched index finger, and the yarn tail over the outstretched thumb of your left hand to make a loop. Both lengths of yarn are held in place by the middle, ring, and pinkie fingers of your left hand. The needle with the slip knot is in the middle of the taut thread you are holding between your thumb and index finger.

Insert the needle from below under the front length of yarn on your thumb.

Pick up the working yarn with your index finger.

Pull the working yarn through the loop on your thumb.

Finally, let the foundation stitch slip from your thumb, and pull the yarn tail taut with your thumb. Lift your thumb again to form the next loop, which can be used to cast on the next stitch. Follow this method to cast on the required number of stitches.

continue on page 29

continue on page 29

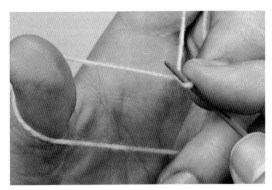

Initial position after making the slip knot

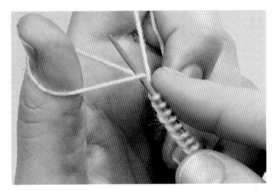

Insert the needle from below under the front thumb yarn.

Thumb cast-on method complete with cuff

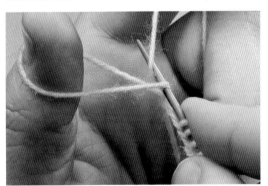

Pick up the working yarn.

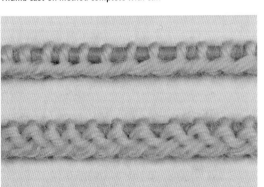

Front (right side) and back (wrong side) of the thumb cast-on method

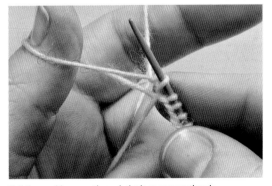

Pull the working yarn through the loop on your thumb.

REINFORCED (OR DOUBLE) THUMB CAST-ON METHOD

If you cast on using the thumb cast-on method with the double yarn over your thumb, the foundation edge is reinforced. It is then very strong yet still stretchy.

For the reinforced, or double, thumb cast-on method, work the slip knot so that the yarn tail is at least eight times as long as the circumference of the sock.

Now fold the yarn over your thumb in half, hold the yarn tail with your right hand, and work the reinforced cast-on using the double yarn over your thumb.

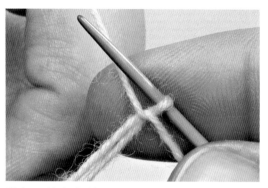

Slip knot with the double yarn

Reinforced (or double) thumb cast-on method with cuff

ELASTIC THUMB CAST-ON METHOD

To get a very elastic cast-on, work the basic thumb cast-on with double the number of stitches. Since this doesn't have a hard edge, this type of cast-on is ideal for those who have poor circulation.

With this cast-on method, the yarn over your thumb must be at least six times as long as the circumference of the sock.

On the first row or round, always work 2 stitches together in order to get to the required number of stitches. This results in a fine, very elastic edge.

Elastic thumb cast-on method with cuff

Tubular (or Italian) Cast-on Method

This method of casting on makes a perfect foundation row that is very elastic. It is perfect to join on to a 1 x 1 rib or a 2 x 2 rib pattern. Since the first row of the tubular cast-on is not very stable, we recommend casting on all the stitches on just one needle and not arranging them equally across four needles until the second row, and then joining this to a round. Unlike the tubular cast-on worked for sweaters, when used for socks, this cast-on method uses the same size needle as you use for the rest of the sock. In order to make the socks more stretchy, you will need to work six transition rounds when knitting the sock.

TUBULAR CAST-ON METHOD WITHOUT A WASTE YARN

A tubular cast-on produces a double layer of fabric. By working all the knit stitches (and slipping the purl stitches), the outside of the sock's foundation row grows by one round. By working all the purl stitches (and slipping the knit stitches), you are forming a round over the inside of the sock's foundation edge. When changing from the cast-on to the cuff pattern, the inner stitches are brought back into the round and the 2 layers of knit fabric are closed, forming a tunnel, or casing.

Work the slip knot so that one yarn tail is at least three times as long as the circumference of the sock.

Hold the needle with the slip knot in your right hand, and the working yarn over the outstretched index finger, and the yarn tail over the outstretched thumb of your left hand. Both lengths of yarn are held in place by the middle finger, ring finger, and pinkie finger of your left hand. The needle with the slip knot is in the middle of the yarn held taut by your thumb and index finger.

Insert the needle from the front underneath the inner thumb thread, pick up the working yarn around your index finger, and bring the loop through below the yarn on your thumb.

Next, insert the needle from above under the yarn on your index finger, pick up the yarn on your thumb, and bring the loop through under the yarn on your index finger.

Repeat both steps until you have the desired number of stitches. It is important that the yarn stays taut, otherwise the stitches will unravel. Do not put this cast-on down.

Note

This method of casting on is the most practical of all the tubular cast-on methods; however, the tension of the yarn cannot be varied much.

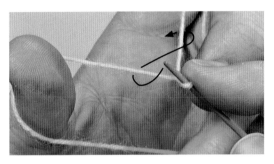

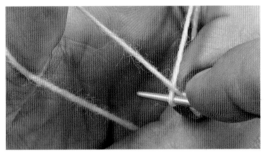

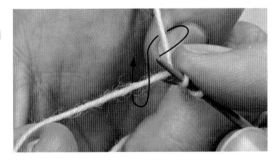

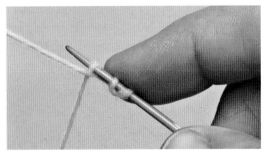

23

Transition to the Cuff

Once you have cast on the given number of stitches, turn the work, then first continue in rows.

Row 1: knit all knit (K) stitches knitwise, slip all purl (P) stitches with the yarn at the front of the work, then turn the work.

Row 2: knit all K stitches knitwise, slip all P stitches with the yarn at the front of the work.

Arrange the stitches evenly across 4 double-pointed needles on this row, join the foundation edge to form a ring, and continue in rounds.

Round 3: purl all P stitches, slip all K stitches with the yarn at the back of the work.

Round 4: knit all K stitches, slip all P stitches with the yarn at the front of the work.

Round 5: purl all P stitches, slip all K stitches with the yarn at the back of the work.

Round 6: knit all K stitches, slip all P stitches with the yarn at the front of the work.

Continue with a 1 x 1 rib or 2 x 2 rib (see page 30, "Rib Cuffs with a Tubular Cast-on").

Tubular cast-on

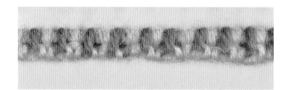

Tubular cast-on with one transition row

Tubular cast-on with six transition rows —3 stitches above one another each on front and back

We have used different colors here to make it easier to see.

Tip

Depending on the thickness of the yarn, the cast-on can be as loose or tight as you want.

TUBULAR CAST-ON METHOD WITH A CROCHETED CHAIN

This method of casting on results in an additional stitch that can be decreased in the following transition rounds. This method is quick and very neat.

To cast on, first crochet a loose chain using a piece of waste yarn, working about 10 stitches more than half the number of stitches required for the foundation row.

Pick up and work 1 stitch into the back side of each chain of the twisted crochet chain (see page 27, "Loop Cast-on Method") and bring the yarn over the needle until you have the required number of stitches on the needle. Be careful not to insert the needle through the waste yarn; otherwise you will not be able to remove the waste yarn later.

To stabilize the last yarn-over, work another stitch into the crocheted chain. This last extra stitch is worked together with the next stitch on the third round when changing to the rib pattern, and is therefore decreased again.

Now work the 6 transition rounds and then a 1 x 1 rib or 2 x 2 rib pattern. Once the cuff is complete, undo the waste yarn, and remove.

Twist the chain cord and pick up the stitches.

Removing the waste yarn

TUBULAR CAST-ON METHOD WITH A WASTE YARN

A tubular cast-on with a piece of waste yarn also results in an additional stitch that is decreased on the transition rounds. It is a bit looser than the tubular cast-on method.

In this variation you cast on the stitches around a piece of waste yarn about 24"/60cm in length. Work the slip knot. The yarn tail should be long enough to weave in at the end. Hold the needle with the slip knot in your right hand. The working yarn is brought over your outstretched index finger. Bring the waste yarn over your outstretched thumb. Your right hand is now holding not only the working needle but both right ends of yarn, while your left hand holds the left end of the waste yarn and the working yarn that comes from the ball.

Insert the needle under the waste yarn and pull through the yarn on your index finger as a stitch, then bring the yarn on your index finger over the waste yarn.

Repeat these two steps until you have the desired number of stitches on the needle. To stabilize the last yarn-over, pull another stitch through under the waste yarn. The additional stitch will be decreased on the third round when changing to the cuff. Then work another 6 transition rounds and a 2 x 2 rib (see page 30, "Rib Cuffs with a Tubular Cast-on"). Remove the waste yarn when the cuff is complete.

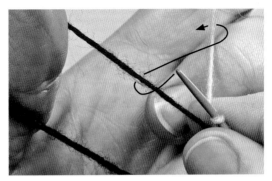
Hold the slip knot and the waste yarn.

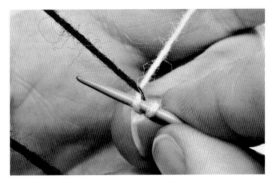
Bring the working yarn under the yarn on the thumb.

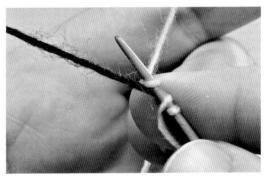
Yarn-over

Changing to the cuff—for both cast-on methods with an additional stitch

Turn the work and continue in rows.

Row 1: Knit all knit (K) stitches knitwise, slip all purl (P) stitches with the yarn at the front of the work, turn the work.

Row 2: Knit all K stitches, slip all P stitches with the yarn at the front of the work.

Arrange the stitches evenly across 4 double-pointed needles on this row, join the foundation edge to form a ring, and continue in rounds.

Round 3: Purl all P stitches purlwise, slip all K stitches with the yarn at the back of the work.

On this round work the last stitch (= the additional stitch) on Needle 4 and the first stitch on Needle 1 together.

Round 4: Knit all K stitches, slip all P stitches with the yarn at the front of the work.

Rounds 5 and 6: Continue as for rounds 3 and 4.

Then continue with a 1 x 1 rib or 2 x 2 rib pattern (see page 30, "Rib Cuffs with a Tubular Cast-on").

Two-Needle Cast-on Method

Often, the cast-on stitches are knitted. These cast-on stitches have to be worked very carefully so that they don't cut in later, as they are not very elastic.

VARIATION 1 (KNITTING ON)

The first variation is similar to the technique used for the French knitting spool since the yarn is pulled through the loop and then brought over the needle.

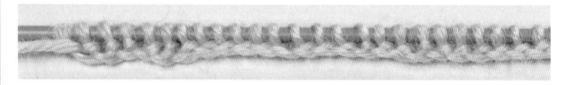

First work the slip knot. The yarn tail should be long enough to weave in at the end.

Hold the needle with the slip knot in your left hand.

With a second needle, work a knit stitch into the basic loop, slip this onto the left-hand needle, and pull up the yarn slightly with your index finger. Now work the next stitch into this new stitch.

Repeat these steps until you have the desired number of stitches on the needle.

Insert into the last loop.

Work off the last loop.

Cast-on with cuff

VARIATION 2 (CABLE CAST-ON)

This method of casting on is a little bit more difficult, but the edge is much neater and is also more elastic.

First work a slip knot with the yarn tail. The yarn tail should be long enough to weave in at the end.

With a second needle work a stitch into this loop, slip the stitch onto the left-hand needle, and pull up slightly. Work all following stitches into the hole between the 2 previous stitches, slip the stitches onto the left-hand needle, and pull up the yarn slightly with your index finger.

Repeat these steps until you have the desired number of stitches on the needle.

Working a stitch into the space between the last 2 stitches

Cast-on with cuff

Loop Cast-on Method

Sometimes it is necessary to continue working in the opposite direction, for example, for heels worked at the end or for double cuffs. This requires a cast-on that allows new stitches to be picked up again. However, loop cast-ons are not very stretchy and are therefore not suited to sock cuffs.

CASTING ON LOOPS

The large loops on the foundation row can be easily picked up with a needle later and worked as stitches. The loop cast-on is especially good for double cuffs since it doesn't ride up too much.

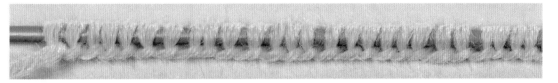

Work as many basic loops as the number of stitches required.

Invisible Cast-on Method

The invisible cast-on blends well into different stitch patterns. Once the crocheted chain has been removed, the open stitches can be picked up and worked, or grafted together. Using a piece of waste yarn, crochet a loose chain using chain stitch. The invisible cast-on is easier to work if you crochet about 10 chain stitches more than the number of stitches required.

Pick up and work new stitches crossways into the back of the chain cord. Make sure you do not insert the needle into the contrasting yarn; otherwise you won't be able to remove the waste yarn easily. Also remember that later you will only be able to pick up one stitch less than you have loops cast on because each loop is staggered by half a stitch, and therefore you "lose" half a stitch at each end.

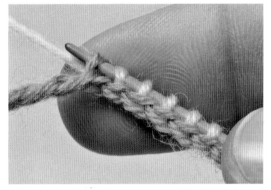

Twist the crocheted chain and pick up the stitches through the back of the chain loops.

Foundation row with knitted rows

Partially unraveled foundation row

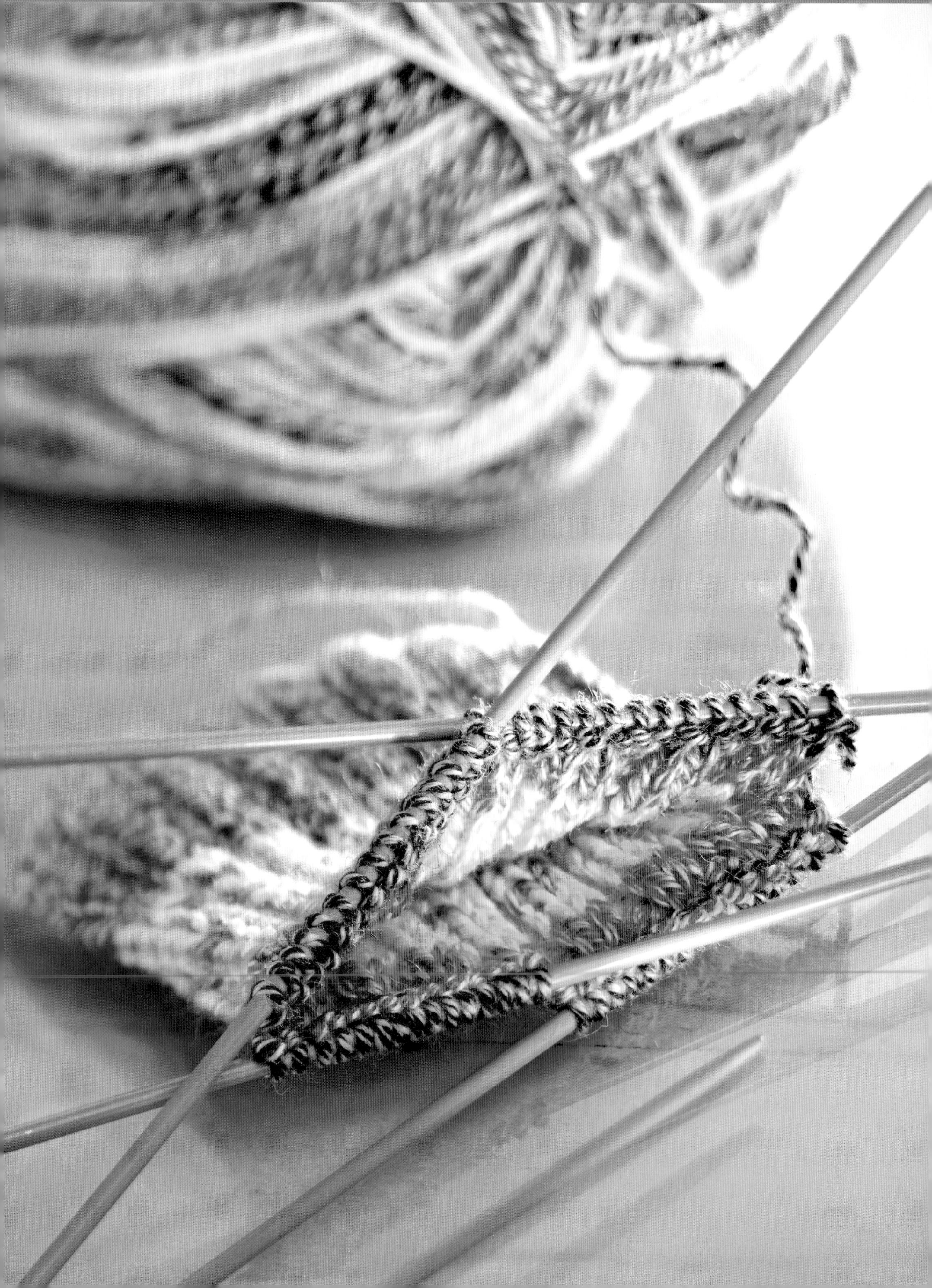

CUFFS

The cuff of a sock has both a decorative and a practical purpose. It keeps the socks elastic around the leg and prevents them from slipping. At the same time it has to be attractive and complement the pattern on the sock.

Ribbed Cuffs

Ribbed cuffs made of knit and purl stitches are very elastic, keeping the sock close up to the leg without being too tight. The elasticity stays even after wearing and washing the socks many times.

1 X 1 (KNIT 1, PURL 1) RIB CUFFS

The 1 x 1 rib cuff is a classic universal cuff that can be combined with almost any pattern.

The number of stitches is a multiple of 2.
   After casting on, work the first row or first round in the following pattern sequence: *knit 1 (K1), purl 1 (P1)*

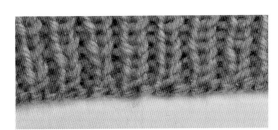

Note

Sequences of stitches between two * are repeated to the end of the row.

Twisted Variation

After casting on, work the first row or round in the following pattern sequence: *K1 through back of loop, P1*
   If you knit the K stitches through the back of the loop, the stitches of the cuff will be tighter and the ribs will be more visible. Insert the needle from right to left through the back part of the stitch when working a K stitch through the back of the loop.

Tip

To determine the height of the cuff, use the number of stitches on one needle as a guide: work as many rounds for the cuff as there are stitches on one needle.

2 X 2 (KNIT 2, PURL 2) RIB CUFF

The 2 x 2 rib is even more popular than the 1 x 1 rib. This might be because it is quicker and easier to knit. But do not work too loosely. This cuff can also be combined with almost any other pattern. The number of stitches should be a multiple of 4, which is usually the case if you are arranging your stitches evenly across 4 double-pointed needles.

After casting on, work the first row or first round in the following pattern sequence:
 K2 through back of loop, P2
   If you need help in avoiding wide holes from forming when you are working P stitches, see page 13 ("Avoiding Holes when Working Purlwise") for more information.

continue on page 35

continue on page 35

29

Twisted Variation

K2 knitwise through back of the loop, P2
   A 2 x 2 rib cuff also becomes tighter when worked with twisted stitches, and the ribs will be more visible.

Ribbed cuffs can be worked with any cast-on method. The diagram shows the difference between the right side (= front) and wrong side (= back) of a cuff worked with knit and purl stitches using the thumb cast-on method. The front (= right side) shows the loops of the cast-on, while on the back (= wrong side) the ridges fit into the rib pattern.

Ribbed Cuffs with a Tubular Cast-on

The tubular cast-on method is ideal for a perfect elastic finish to all ribbed cuffs. The ribbed cuffs are joined on to the six transition rounds that you already work for the tubular cast-on method.

1 X 1 RIB CUFF WITH A TUBULAR CAST-ON

The number of stitches is a multiple of 2.
   After the transition rounds of the tubular cast-on method, work all knit (K) stitches knitwise and all purl (P) stitches purlwise.

CUFF WITH A TUBULAR CAST-ON

The number of stitches is a multiple of 4.
   After the transition rounds of the tubular cast-on method, continue as follows until all the stitches of the first round of the cuff have been worked:
   knit 1 stitch knitwise, slip 1 stitch, loosen the next knit stitch slightly and knit, leaving the stitch on the needle, purl the slipped stitch, and slip both stitches off the left-hand needle, purl 1
   Then work a 2 x 2 rib cuff.

Garter Cuffs

The garter cuff is a decorative cuff. It stretches well but does not spring back together. It is a perfect finish for all scalloped and chevron patterns that are already elastic in themselves.

After casting on, work the rounds alternately purlwise and knitwise to create the uneven appearance. The wrong side of the thumb cast-on method looks good with the rib pattern.

TWISTED GARTER CUFF

An unusual variation of the garter cuff is the twisted garter cuff. This is worked first on two needles in garter stitch flat (back and forth). It is joined to form a ring on the row after it has been twisted. Usually a rib pattern is joined onto the garter edge so that the twisted cuff looks more like a decorative finish to a cuff.

Garter stitch: 6 rows in 3 colors

After casting on the required number of stitches, work the first 5 rows in garter stitch (in our example we have used three colors). Cast on with one color and then work one more row in this color, then work 2 rows in garter stitch with each of the other two colors. Then continue knitwise in the color of the cuff, twisting the right-hand needle once around the edge of the cuff after 4 stitches. Repeat this twist every 4 stitches. At the end of the row turn and work the stitches in reverse cuff pattern. Turn once more, then arrange the cuff stitches evenly across 4 double-pointed needles and join to a round.

Twisted row: one row, half a twist with right-hand needle below

It is also possible to work any number of stitches between the twist stitches. But you will have to make sure that the number of stitches can be divided evenly.

Now continue with the cuff itself—usually this will be a twisted rib pattern. The twisted garter cuff looks especially good if it includes colors that will later be included in the leg.

Twisted row: after twisting, continue knitwise.

The finished cuff

Double Cuffs

The double cuff is especially decorative when used on women's and children's socks. It doesn't get tight but remains elastic when the foundation edge is knitted as shown here. If you sew the foundation edge in position at the end, it loses its elasticity.

The principle of the double cuff applies to all variations shown here. Cast on the required number of stitches using either the loop cast-on method, page 27, (this will give you large foundation stitches that can easily be picked up by a second needle) or the invisible cast-on method, also page 27, then join to form a ring.

Work the cuff to the desired height in stockinette stitch—in general this will be 6 to 10 rounds. Now work a fold edging. The variations shown here give you different forms. Then continue again in stockinette stitch, working one round more than on the inside.

Turn the foundation edge in so that the fold edging forms the lower finish.

Now each stitch can be worked together with its foundation loop. Pick up the loops with a spare set of double-pointed needles and knit each stitch together with a loop. If you use the yarn tail (at the start of the round) as your guide, the stitch and the foundation loop should be directly above each other.

Double cuff, lower and upper panel, with an eyelet round as the fold edging in the middle

Double cuff knitted on the foundation edge

Knit double cuff and foundation edge together.

Tip

The outer rounds, worked in stockinette stitch, make a lovely panel that can be decorated with beads, embroidery, or stripes.

SIMPLE FOLD EDGING

The simple fold edging can be worked over any number of stitches. Simply purl the fold edging round.

CLASSIC PICOT EDGING

The number of stitches is a multiple of 2.
  Work the fold edging round as follows:
  knit 2 stitches together, yarn-over
  On the following round work all the stitches and yarn-overs in stockinette stitch.

SCALLOPED EDGING

The number of stitches is a multiple of 4.
  Work the fold edging round as follows:
  yarn-over, slip 2 stitches and work together (left slanting), work 2 stitches together (right slanting), yarn-over
  On the following round knit all stitches, and first knit the two adjoining yarn-overs and then knit them again through the back of the loops.

Frilly Cuffs

Frilly cuffs are a lovely finish for women's or children's socks. They stretch well but only become really elastic through the adjoining ribbed cuff.

To make a frilly cuff, cast on three times as many stitches using the thumb cast-on method, then work 10 rounds in stockinette stitch.
  Reduce the number of stitches by working 3 stitches together throughout on the next round. On the following round, continue working the ribbed cuff.

Example

For a cuff requiring 60 stitches, first cast on 180 stitches and work 10 rounds either on 8"/20cm double-pointed needles or on a 16"/40cm circular needle.

Rolled Cuffs

Rolled cuffs are a lovely finish on women's or children's socks. They stretch well but only become really elastic through the ribbed cuff. They look especially good when worked in different colors.

Cast on the required number of stitches and work 12 rounds in stockinette stitch. If several rolled edgings are to be worked one above the other, work each one separately on double-pointed needles for about 4 to 6 rounds more than the previous one.

Finally, insert one rolled edging inside the other—the rolled edging with the most rounds is on the inside—and work the stitches on all double-pointed needles together.

In our example, knit the first stitch of the yellow rolled edging and the first stitch of the orange rolled edging together, and so on.

To work the stitches of 3 rolled edgings together, it is best to work the stitches of the two inner rolled edgings together first. This is done by alternately knitting 1 stitch of the center rolled edging and 1 stitch of the longer rolled edging together. On the next round, add the stitches of the shorter rolled edging to the others.

A twisted 1 x 1 rib cuff makes the rolled edging really elastic.

Two separate rolled edgings

Two rolled edgings, one inside the other

Rolled edgings with twisted rib cuff

The Leg

Once the cast-on and cuff give the sock a good fit, it continues with the leg. The leg is worked in rounds without any increases or decreases. There is plenty of room here for creativity in terms of designs, textured patterns, cables, eyelets, or multicolored designs, all of which would look really great. See page 118 for detailed instructions on converting patterns for rows into patterns for rounds. However, many self-patterning yarns can simply be worked in stockinette stitch and will still look great.

   To make the stockinette stitch leg even more elastic, you could work a "stretch gusset" into the sock by working the last stitch on every needle purlwise. This gusset can also be continued along the foot. For generations, the recommendation was to work the leg the same length as measured from the ball of your thumb to the top of your middle finger. While this is a good guide, obviously the wearer's taste and what the socks are to be used for also play a role. Socks that are to be worn in boots obviously have to be worked higher than summer socks. The height of the leg is also dependent on the pattern and its motif. Frequently ½"/ 1⅓ cm to 1"/ 2½ cm more or less can make that sock look really special.

continue
on page 53

continue
on page 48

HEELS

A good fit is especially important when it comes to the heel. That's why it is the most important part of any pair of socks. For this chapter we reviewed and evaluated a wide variety of heels both technically and visually. The result is a great collection of methods for working heels that can quickly be adjusted to fit the size and width of any foot.

Fitting the Heel

The knitted heel protects a very sensitive part of your foot but is also subject to a lot of wear and tear. If it is too wide around the instep, the sock will crease in the shoe. However, if it is too tight around the instep, the whole sock will become distorted and will pull around the foot in order to get more room.

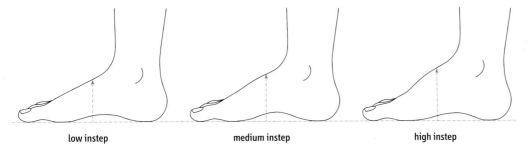

| low instep | medium instep | high instep |

The width of the foot should determine the direction of the heel seams. These seams form the rounding of the heel and make the sock fit the foot. The seams should only run along suitable places where they are not subject to a lot of pressure. If the sock presses or rubs on the foot, it will be uncomfortable and can cause the skin to chafe. On the other hand, if the shoe rubs too much on the heel seam, it can open up or wear through.

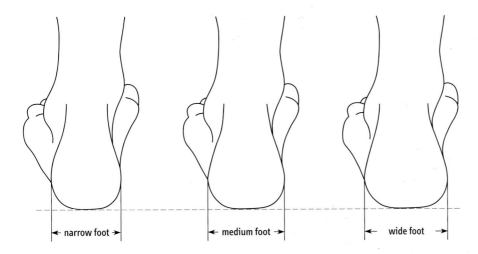

| ← narrow foot → | ← medium foot → | ← wide foot → |

A correct fit is necessary if the socks are to be comfortable and last a long time. For generations, instructions on working the heel have always included tips on improving the fit. As a result, it is said that men's feet need heel flaps and women's feet need heels with short rows. But this has never been proven to be true.

Note

On the whole, knitted fabric is quite elastic, so small discrepancies in the fit are compensated for easily. However, the less elastic the pattern of the upper foot, the more important it is to get the heel right.

FINDING THE RIGHT HEEL

WIDTH OF HEEL	HEIGHT OF INSTEP	HEEL FORM
narrow	low	short-row heel, short-row heel with reinforced double stitches, wrap stitch heel, mock short-row heel
	medium	diagonal-seam heel with increase and decrease gusset
	high	standard (square) heel, hybrid heel
medium	low	rounded short-row heel
	medium	standard (square) heel, "afterthought" heel
	high	horseshoe heel, standard (square) heel
wide	low	round short-row heel
	medium	round heel
	high	heart-shaped heel

Tips on Working the Heel

It's worth keeping a few things in mind before working the heel in order to avoid any mishaps.

KEEPING TRACK OF THE NEEDLES

Each round starts with Needle 1, clearly recognizable by the yarn tail. Start counting needles from this tail in the direction in which you are working the knit piece.

In general when working heels flat (back and forth), they are worked over the stitches on Needles 4 and 1, also called the heel stitches. Again, start the heel at the center of a row—in other words, between Needles 4 and 1. The heel starts and ends with a half row.

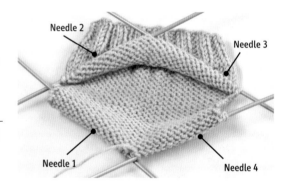

LEAVING THE STITCHES ON NEEDLES 2 AND 3 ON ONE SIDE

If you move your hands only slightly, the stitches can stay on the double-pointed needles.

There is more room to work if you arrange the stitches evenly across 3 instead of across 2 needles. This is especially helpful if you are leaving one of the double-pointed needles on one side anyway.

But it is much easier if you slip the stitches to be left on one side onto the flexible center cable of a circular needle.

INCREASING THROUGH THE HORIZONTAL STRAND

Pick up the horizontal strand between 2 stitches. Twist the strand and slip it onto the left-hand needle, then work through the back of the loop. The twisting avoids small holes from forming.

Picking up the horizontal strand

Twist the strand and knit.

AVOIDING HOLES

Sometimes small but unsightly holes can appear along the sides between the heel and upper foot on the first round after picking up stitches along heel flap selvages or after working short rows. Any attempt to try to avoid this by working the stitches tighter is usually useless. These holes are usually caused by the fact that some people pull up the stitches on the left-hand needle very high when they work them. If all the stitches are worked like this, you carry the yarn of the previous round slightly forward. In general, this results in a very even stitch pattern. However, problems arise where the horizontal strand of the previous round has been blocked from being carried across, as in the case of the rounds worked between Needles 1 and 2 and even more between Needles 3 and 4. The last stitch then appears much bigger than all the others.

To reduce such holes when changing from one needle to another, the horizontal strand has to be shortened slightly. To do this, pick up the horizontal strand between Needles 1 and 2, twist it once, and knit it and the first stitch on Needle 2 together. On the other side, pick up the horizontal strand between Needles 3 and 4, twist it, and knit it and the last stitch on Needle 3 together—in other words, with the outer stitches of the upper foot.

The twisted horizontal strand can also be worked with the 2 outer heel stitches—in other words, with the last stitch on Needle 1 and the first stitch on Needle 4.

For an even stitch pattern, decide whether to work together the outer stitches of the upper foot or the outer stitches of the heel, but do not mix them.

Depending on the technique used, heels can be divided into three different types:

- heels with heel flaps and gusset: this includes all types of turning heels
- heels with diagonal seams: all heels worked with short rows
- round heels that end on the heel: either worked on at the end or straight in

HEELS WITH HEEL FLAPS

The heel flap covers the heel at the back from the start of the ankle to the lower end of the heel. It is worked flat (back and forth) over half of the stitches. Heels with heel flaps start relatively high up and provide the instep with a lot of space. Turning the heel joins the heel flap with the sole, creating a small indentation for the lower end of the heel—the "kink" in the sock. In order to continue working in rounds at the base of the heel, you will need to pick up stitches along the double-beaded selvage of both sides of the heel flap. The extra stitches are decreased on the following rounds. These decreases form a very characteristic stitch triangle—the gusset.

Among the types of heels with heel flap are:

- the standard (square) heel turned over 3 panels
- the horseshoe heel turned over 4 panels
- the heart-shaped heel turned over 2 panels
- the round heel

SHAPE OF THE HEEL WITH HEEL FLAPS

The four heel shapes shown here vary in their rounded shape: square (standard), horseshoe, heart, and round. Different methods of turning the heel result in very different heel shapes. The standard heel turned on 3 needles forms a square heel shape. The horseshoe heel is rounded with straight sides forming a horseshoe, giving the heel more space than the standard heel. The heart forms a triangular heel, also described as V-shaped, rather like the lower part of a heart. The heart can be used to create even more width for the heel. The round heel, with its side decreases, forms a rectangle; the width is comparable to that of a standard heel, but because the rows are worked completely, it is more suitable for wider feet.

Standard (square) heel

Horseshoe heel

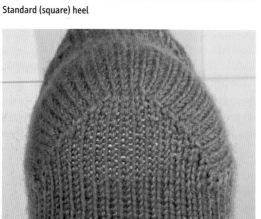
Heart-shaped heel

Round heel

Tips on Working a Heel Flap

The heel flaps for all four types of heels are worked much the same. Therefore, we have included a few important things to be aware of to make working them easier.

DOUBLE-BEADED SELVAGE

The first and last stitches of each row are called selvage stitches. For a double-beaded selvage, work both selvage stitches at each end knitwise both on the right-side and on the wrong-side rows. Note that if the first stitch of each row was simply slipped without being worked, this would lead to an edge with large stitches, resulting in holes at the side of the heel later.

By working the selvage stitches "double," the stitches become very close and firm. Small knots, or beads, form at each end, marking every second row. By working the beads, you avoid holes from forming, and the change to the new round of stitches becomes less noticeable. Also, the beads make it easier to count the number of completed rows.

PICKING UP NEW STITCHES ALONG THE DOUBLE-BEADED SELVAGE

The new stitches that are picked up along the double-beaded selvage will be uniform if you work 1 stitch into each bead.

To do this, insert the right-hand needle into the next bead and pull through a new stitch. This way you are picking up 1 stitch for every 2 rows.

According to the 3-to-4 rule, picking up 3 stitches for every 4 rows of the heel flap makes the panels fit together better. But here there are only 2 new stitches for 4 selvage stitches. the yarn for the new row of stitches becomes a little shorter than it should be with the result that the first picked-up row of stitches is tighter, and so there are no small holes in the sides.

Picking up new stitches on right-side rows

Picking up new stitches on wrong-side rows

Tip

To avoid a hole created by wide stitches from appearing in the center of the heel, slip the stitches from Needles 1 and 4 onto one needle. When the heel flap is complete, rearrange these stitches on 2 double-pointed needles again.

Note

For a stronger heel flap, knit the first and last 2 or 3 stitches knitwise (= garter stitch). The short ribs at each end make the rows easier to count; plus the small pattern on the sides looks good.

REINFORCING THE HEEL

Heel flaps are under considerable strain when the socks are worn in shoes. To prevent the knit fabric in the heel flaps from getting thinner with wear, the heel flap can be reinforced or made thicker than the rest of the sock. The easiest way to do this is by incorporating a second, matching yarn into the knitting when making the heel flap and turning the heel. Slipped stitch patterns are very popular for this and can be incorporated into the reinforced ribbing above one another or worked in on alternate rows for overall reinforcement.

These patterns are worked by slipping every second knit stitch unworked onto the right-hand needle on right-side rows and carrying the yarn not in use loosely across at the back of the work; on the wrong-side rows, the stitches are purled as usual. This leaves a stranded yarn behind the stitch, thereby thickening the stitch.

Reinforced Ribs

Row 1 (right-side row): Selvage stitch, *knit 1, slip 1*, selvage stitch.

Row 2 (wrong-side row): Selvage stitch, purl all stitches, selvage stitch.

Repeat these two rows until you have reached the required height.

Reinforced Netting

Row 1 (right-side row): Selvage stitch, *knit 1, slip 1*, selvage stitch.

Row 2 (wrong-side row): Selvage stitch, purl all stitches, selvage stitch.

Row 3 (right-side row): Selvage stitch, slip 1, knit 1, selvage stitch.

Row 4 (wrong-side row): Selvage stitch, purl all stitches, selvage stitch.

Repeat these 4 rows until you have reached the required height.

Interwoven Reinforcement

The advantage of weaving in a length of yarn is that it is possible to reinforce a heel afterward. Ideally, this is done using a second baby (3-ply) or fingering-weight (4-ply) yarn. Using a blunt darning or embroidery needle, always weave the yarn on the inside of the heel through the crossways loops of the purl stitches vertical to the rows. The woven-in yarn is not visible on the right side of the work.

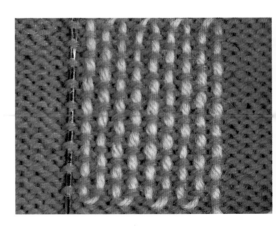

Turning a Heel over 3 Panels
. . . narrow heel, high instep

The three-panel heel turn is a classic method, and the most popular means of turning the heel for many generations of knitters. Its particular advantage is that it is easy to work and there are plenty of possibilities for incorporating extra strength.

THE HEEL FLAP

Leave the stitches on Needles 2 and 3 on one side. Slip the stitches on Needles 4 and 1 onto one double-pointed needle and work the heel flap in open rows, working the selvage stitches as double-beaded stitches (= knit the first and last stitch of every row). The heel flap is the right height when there are half as many beads on either side as there are stitches on the needle for the heel, or—and this is the same thing—as many beads as there are stitches on one needle.

End the heel with half of a right-side row at the center of the heel.

TURNING A HEEL

To turn a heel, work back and forth over the center stitches of the heel flap. Rearrange the needles as follows: slip the stitches on Needles 2 and 3 from the holder onto one double-pointed needle. This is necessary because the heel flap has now grown considerably and the stitches on the holder hardly have any room to move when knitted.

In your mind, arrange the heel stitches into 3 sections: two equal side panels and one center panel.

If the number of stitches is not divisible by three, put the rest of the stitches on the center panel needle. The stitch arrangement for all sizes is given in the chart below. The figure between the slashes (/) is the number of stitches of the center panel; the two outer figures are the number of stitches on either side.

Pick up the correct number of stitches along both sides of the heel flap with one of the free double-pointed needles to fit the desired size of sock.

Starting point for the heel flap:
Arrange the stitches into two side panels and one center panel.

NUMBER OF STITCHES FOR TURNING A HEEL WITH FINGERING/4-PLY SOCK YARN
1¾ oz./50g, 229 yards/210m, 30 stitches x 42 rows = 4"/10cm

Children's and women's sizes	5/5½	6/7	8/9	9½/10	11/11½	12/13	1/2	3/4	5/6	7/8	9/9½	10/11	12/13	14/15
Men's sizes										5/6	7/8	9/10	11/12	13/14
Continental sizes	20/21	22/23	24/25	26/27	28/29	30/31	32/33	34/35	36/37	38/39	40/41	42/43	44/45	46/47
Total stitches/per needle	44/11	44/11	48/12	48/12	52/13	52/13	56/14	56/14	60/15	60/15	64/16	64/16	68/17	68/17
Total stitches per heel	22	22	24	24	26	26	28	28	30	30	32	32	34	36
Heel flap arrangement	7/8/7		8/8/8		8/10/8		9/10/9		10/10/10		10/12/10		11/12/11	12/12/12

Note

Empty squares in the chart indicate that the figures are the same as those in the box to the left.

Note

This is where the more advanced knitters can give the socks a more professional fit by working more or fewer stitches at the center. But remember that the panels on either side must have the same number of stitches!

Tip

If the heel flap is to be reinforced, add the extra strength by working the slip stitches across the right-side rows in pattern, either by working in a second yarn or by weaving it in at the end.

NUMBER OF STITCHES FOR TURNING A HEEL WITH DK/6-PLY SOCK YARN
1¾ oz./50g, 136 yards/125m, 22 stitches x 30 rows to 4"/10cm

Children's and women's sizes	5/5½	6/7	8/9	9½/10	11/11½	12/13	1/2	3/4	5/6	7/8	9/9½	10/11	12/13	14/15
Men's sizes										5/6	7/8	9/10	11/12	13/14
Continental sizes	20/21	22/23	24/25	26/27	28/29	30/31	32/33	34/35	36/37	38/39	40/41	42/43	44/45	46/47
Total stitches per needle	32/8	32/8	36/9	36/9	40/10	40/10	44/11	44/11	48/12	48/12	52/13	52/13	52/13	56/14
Total stitches per heel	16	16	18	18	20	20	22	22	24	24	26	26	26	28
Heel flap arrangement	5/6/5		6/6/6		6/8/6		7/8/7		8/8/8		8/10/8			9/10/9

Start at the center of the heel on a right-side row. The side panels are left on the side, each on a separate needle; the center panel has been half worked. The heel is worked over the stitches of the center panel only.

Row 1 (½ right-side row): Work in stockinette stitch, slip the last stitch of the center panel, leave the needle on one side, slip the first stitch of the side panel, knit both stitches together (left slanting), turn.

Row 2 (wrong-side row): Slip the first stitch with the needle that was left on one side, purl the stitches of the center panel, slip the last stitch of the center panel, leave the needle on one side, slip the slipped stitch onto the left-hand needle, purl both stitches together, and turn.

Row 3 (right-side row): Slip the first stitch with the needle that was left on one side, knit the stitches of the center panel, slip the last stitch of the center panel, leave the needle on one side, slip the first stitch of the side panel, knit both stitches together (left slanting), turn.

Repeat rows 2 and 3, slipping the first stitch of every row and working the last stitch together with the next stitch of the side panel until there are no more stitches on the side panels and only the stitches of the center panel remain on the needle.

End the heel with half a right-side row at the center.

Knit the last stitch of the center panel together with the first stitch of the side panel.

PICKING UP STITCHES AND THE GUSSET

Once the heel is turned, continue working in rounds and, at the same time, on the first round, pick up new stitches along the double-beaded selvage on either side of the heel flap (= 1 stitch into each bead).

Work one more round over all the needles for the sole: work the stitches on Needles 2 and 3 in pattern and those on Needles 1 and 4 in stockinette stitch. Arrange the stitches on Needles 4 and 1 so that there are the same number of stitches on both needles. Then mark the round change between Needle 4 to Needle 1.

To avoid side holes, pick up the horizontal strand between the heel and the upper foot on either side on this round, slip it twisted onto the needle, and knit it together with the outer stitches of the upper foot (= the first stitch on Needle 2 and the last stitch on Needle 3) or with the outer stitches of the heel (= the last stitch on Needle 1 and the first stitch on Needle 4).

The decreases worked for the gusset have not yet eliminated all the extra stitches so that you are back to the original number. This gives the gusset more room in the instep. On the following rounds, the number of stitches for the gusset is gradually reduced to the original number.

Begin at the start of the round for Needle 1. After picking up the stitches along the side of the heel flap, you have already worked one round.

DECREASE ROUND

Knit all the stitches on Needle 1, work to 3 stitches from the end of Needle 1 and knit the next 2 stitches together (right slanting), knit 1. Work the stitches on Needles 2 and 3 in pattern, knit all the stitches on Needle 4, slipping the second and third stitches and knit both stitches together (left slanting).

Repeat this decrease round every second or third round until you have the same number of stitches on the heel needles as you had at the beginning.

Then continue in rounds for the foot.

Repeat the gusset decreases on every second or third round.

Turning a Horseshoe Heel over 4 Panels
... medium heel, high instep

The horseshoe heel combines the standard (square) heel with a few short rows, thereby creating a wider heel than the heel with a gusset. Since the horseshoe is wider than the gusset, requiring fewer decreases, more gusset stitches need to be decreased. This makes the gusset triangle bigger.

Tip

The horseshoe heel requires an additional stitch marker; you can use either a paper clip or a length of waste yarn.

THE HEEL FLAP

Slip the stitches on Needles 2 and 3 onto a stitch holder.

Slip the stitches on Needles 4 and 1 onto one needle and work the heel flap back and forth, working the selvage stitches as double-beaded stitches (= knit the first and last stitch of every row). The heel flap is the right height when there are half as many beads on either side as there are stitches on the needle for the heel, or—and this is the same thing—as many beads as there are stitches on one needle.

End the heel with half a right-side row at the center of the heel.

HORSESHOE GUSSET

The horseshoe gusset is worked back and forth over the center stitches of the heel flap only and combines short rows (horseshoe shaping) with the standard gusset (straight sides).

Pick up the stitches on Needles 2 and 3 and slip them onto one needle.

Arrange the heel stitches on four needles: two equal side panels and two equal center panels. The stitch arrangement for all sizes is given in the charts on page 46. The figures between the slashes (/) are the number of stitches of the two center panels; the two outer figures are the number of stitches on either side.

Pick up the correct number of stitches along both sides of the heel flap with one of the free double-pointed needles in the correct size. Mark the center of the heel by placing a stitch marker or a paper clip on the right-hand needle or inserting a piece of waste yarn between the needles.

Starting point for working the horseshoe gusset: arrange the stitches over two side panels and two center panels.

NUMBER OF STITCHES FOR HORSESHOE GUSSET WITH FINGERING/4-PLY SOCK YARN

1³/₄ oz./50g, 230 yards/210m, 30 stitches x 42 rows = 4"/10cm

Children's and women's sizes	5/5½	6/7	8/9	9½/10	11/11½	12/13	1/2	3/4	5/6	7/8	9/9½	10/11	12/13	14/15
Men's sizes										5/6	7/8	9/10	11/12	13/14
Continental sizes	20/21	22/23	24/25	26/27	28/29	30/31	32/33	34/35	36/37	38/39	40/41	42/43	44/45	46/47
Total stitches/per needle	40/11	44/11	48/12	48/12	52/13	52/13	56/14	56/14	60/15	60/15	64/16	64/16	68/17	72/18
Total stitches per heel	22	22	24	24	26	26	28	28	30	30	32	32	34	34
Heel flap arrangement	5/6/6/5		6/6/6/6		7/6/6/7		8/6/6/8	6/8/8/6	7/8/8/7		8/8/8/8		9/8/8/9	10/8/8/10
Central stitches	3							4						5

NUMBER OF STITCHES FOR HORSESHOE GUSSET WITH DK/6-PLY SOCK YARN

1³/₄ oz./50g, 137 yards/125m, 22 stitches x 30 rows to 4"/10cm

Children's and women's sizes	5/5½	6/7	8/9	9½/10	11/11½	12/13	1/2	3/4	5/6	7/8	9/9½	10/11	12/13	14/15
Men's sizes										5/6	7/8	9/10	11/12	13/14
Continental sizes	20/21	22/23	24/25	26/27	28/29	30/31	32/33	34/35	36/37	38/39	40/41	42/43	44/45	46/47
Total stitches/per needle	32/8	32/8	36/9	36/9	40/10	40/10	44/11	44/11	48/12	48/12	52/13	52/13	52/13	56/14
Total stitches per heel	16	16	18	18	20	20	22	22	24	24	26	26	26	28
Heel flap arrangement	4/4/4/4		5/4/4/5		6/4/4/6		6/5/5/6	6/6/6/6	7/6/6/7		7/6/6/7			7/7/7/7
Central stitches	2							3						4

Tip

If you have some experience working with short rows, you can also work the selvage stitches of the horseshoe as double-beaded stitches or wrap stitches (see page 53, "Working Double Stitches," and page 58, "Working Wrap Stitches").

ROUNDED HORSESHOE SHAPE

Start at the center of the heel on a right-side row. The side panels are left on the side, each on a separate needle; the center panel has been half worked. The center of the heel has been marked.

Row 1 (¹/₂ right-side row): Knit the stitches of the rounded edge (= half the stitches of the first center panel) and turn.

Row 2 (wrong-side row): Slip the first stitch purlwise, purl to the center, remove the stitch marker, purl the number of central stitches (= half the stitches of the second center panel) past the center again, turn.

Row 3 (right-side row): Slip the first stitch knitwise, knit all the stitches, including the slipped stitch of the row below (recognizable by the slightly larger hole between the stitches—see photograph), knit 1 more stitch, turn.

Row 4 (wrong-side row): Slip the first stitch purlwise, purl to the slipped stitch of the row below, purl 1 more stitch, turn.

Repeat rows 3 and 4, working 1 more stitch into the horseshoe on every row until the rounded section of the horseshoe has been worked over all center panel stitches.
    End with one complete wrong-side row.

On the left-hand needle are (seen from the right side) the slipped stitch of the previous row, the hole, and the as-yet-unworked center panel stitches.

HORSESHOE LEG

On all following rows, slip the first stitch of every row as you did when turning the heel the standard way, and working the last stitch together with the next stitch of the side panel until there are no more side panel stitches and only the stitches of the center panel remain.

Row 1 (right-side row): Slip the first stitch, knit all the stitches of the center panel, slip the last stitch of the center panel, leave the needle on one side, slip the first stitch of the side panel and knit both stitches together (left slanting), turn.

Row 2 (wrong-side row): Slip the first stitch on the needle that was left on one side, purl all the stitches of the center panel to 1 stitch from the end of the needle, slip the last stitch of the center panel, leave the needle on one side, slip the last stitch onto the left-hand needle and purl both stitches together, turn.

Repeat rows 1 and 2 until only the horseshoe stitches remain on the needle.
End with half a right-side row.

PICKING UP STITCHES AND THE GUSSET

Once the heel is turned, continue working in rounds and, at the same time, on the first round, pick up new stitches along the double-beaded selvage on either side of the heel flap (= 1 stitch for each bead).

Work one more round over all the needles for the sole: work the stitches on Needles 2 and 3 in pattern and those on Needles 1 and 4 in stockinette stitch. Arrange the stitches on Needles 4 and 1 so that there are the same number of stitches on both needles. Then mark the round change between Needles 4 and 1.

To avoid side holes, pick up the horizontal strand between the heel and the upper foot on either side on this round, slip it twisted onto the needle, and knit it together with the outer stitches of the upper foot (= the first stitch on Needle 2 and the last stitch on Needle 3) or with the outer stitches of the heel (= the last stitch on Needle 1 and the first stitch on Needle 4).

The decreases worked for the gusset have not yet eliminated all the extra stitches so that you are back to the original number. On the following rounds, the number of stitches for the gusset is gradually reduced to the original number.

Begin at the start of the round for Needle 1. After picking up the stitches along the side of the heel flap, you have already worked one round.

DECREASE ROUND

Knit all the stitches on Needle 1, work to 3 stitches from the end of Needle 1 and knit the next 2 stitches together (right slanting), knit 1. Work the stitches on Needles 2 and 3 in pattern, knit all the stitches on Needle 4, slipping the second and third stitches and knit both stitches together (left slanting).

Repeat this decrease round every 2 rounds until you have the same number of stitches on the heel needles as you had at the beginning.
Then continue in rounds for the foot.

Note

If the horseshoe heel is to be reinforced, add the extra strength either by working in a second yarn or by weaving it in at the end (see page 42, "Reinforcing the Heel"). Those important selvage stitches of the short rows only rarely benefit from reinforced slipped stitches.

continue
on page 49

Turning a Heart-Shaped Heel over 2 Panels
. . . wide foot, high instep

The heart shape has the widest heel and therefore has the least decreases when turning the heel, but it needs the most gusset decreases. It is easy to work and, in comparison to the other heel flaps, does not need much counting. The heart-shaped heel also provides narrower feet with a comfortable slipper.

Note

If the heel flap is to be reinforced, add the extra strength either by working in a second yarn or by weaving it in at the end (see page 42, "Reinforcing the Heel"). Those important selvage stitches of the short rows only rarely benefit from reinforced slipped stitches.

HEEL FLAP

Leave the stitches on Needles 2 and 3 on a holder. Slip the stitches on Needles 4 and 1 onto one double-pointed needle and work the heel flap back and forth, working the selvage stitches as a double-beaded edge (= knit first and last stitch of every row).

HEART

Work the heart in rows over just the center stitches of the heel flap. Start the heel at the center of a right-side row. The stitches are evenly distributed across 4 double-pointed needles.

Row 1 (½ right-side row): Slip the first stitch knitwise, slip 2 stitches and knit both stitches together (left slanting), knit 1 more stitch, turn.

Row 2 (wrong-side row): Slip the first stitch purlwise, purl 3 stitches, purl 2 stitches together, purl 1 more stitch, turn.

Row 3 (right-side row): Slip the first stitch knitwise, knit 4 stitches to the slipped stitch of the previous row, slip 2 stitches, knit 2 stitches together (left slanting), knit 1 more stitch, turn.

Row 4 (wrong-side row): Slip the first stitch purlwise, purl 5 stitches to the slipped stitch of the previous row, purl 2 stitches together, purl 1 more stitch, turn.

On the following rows, continue over the center heel stitches. At the same time, slip the first stitch, work to the slipped stitch of the previous row, work this stitch together with the next side panel stitch, work 1 more stitch, turn. This way the heart grows by 1 stitch on every row until all stitches of the side panels have been worked into the heart. The V-shape of the lower heart is clearly recognizable when turning the heel.

The heel flap has the right height when there are half as many beads at both edges as there are heel stitches—and this is the same—when there are as many beads on one double-pointed needle as there are stitches. End with half a right side row at the center of the heel.

As seen from the right side of work, the left needle can now be seen with the slipped stitch of the previous row, the gap between the stitches, and the still unworked heart stitches.

PICKING UP STITCHES AND GUSSET

Once the heart is complete, continue working in rounds and, at the same time, on the first round, pick up new stitches along the double-beaded selvage on either side of the heel flap (= 1 stitch for each bead).

Work 1 more round over all the needles for the sole: work the stitches on Needles 2 and 3 in pattern and those on Needles 1 and 4 in stockinette stitch. Arrange the stitches on Needles 4 and 1 so that there are the same number of stitches on both needles. Then mark the round change between Needles 4 and 1.

To avoid side holes, pick up the horizontal strand between the heel and the upper foot on either side of this round, slip it twisted onto the needle, and knit it together with the outer stitches of the upper foot (= the first stitch on Needle 2 and the last stitch on Needle 3) or with the outer stitches of the heel (= the last stitch on Needle 1 and the first stitch on Needle 4).

The decreases worked for the gussett have not yet eliminated all the extra stitches so that you are back to the original number. On the following rounds, the number of stitches for the heart is gradually reduced to the original number.

Begin at the start of the round for Needle 1. After picking up the stitches along the side of the heel flap, you have already worked one round.

DECREASE ROUND

Knit all the stitches on Needle 1, work to 3 stitches from the end of Needle 1 and knit the next 2 stitches together (right slanting), knit 1. Work the stitches on Needles 2 and 3 in pattern, knit all the stitches on Needle 4, slipping the second and third stitches and knitting both stitches together (left slanting).

Repeat this decrease round every 2 rounds until you have the same number of stitches on the heel needles as you had at the beginning.

Continue in rounds for the foot.

continue on page 71

Round Heel

. . . wide heel, medium instep

Turning this heel is always done in complete rows, without any short rows at all. The round heel is a neat alternative for beginning sock knitters and all those who are not comfortable with short rows.

Working a round heel is a lot easier if you use two stitch markers or paper clips.

HEEL FLAP

Leave the stitches on Needles 2 and 3 on one side.

Slip the stitches on Needles 4 and 1 onto one needle and work the heel flap back and forth, working the selvage stitches as double-beaded stitches (= knit the first and last stitch of every row). The heel flap is the right height when there are half as many beads on either side as there are stitches on the needle for the heel, or—and this is the same thing—as many beads as there are stitches on one needle. If there is an odd number of stitches, work 1 more bead.

The heel flap of the round heel is worked half as high as any other heel flap.

TURNING A HEEL

Pick up the stitches on Needles 2 and 3, slip them onto one needle, and leave the needle on one side; this will create a free double-pointed needle.

Unlike the other gussets, the heel of the rounded heel is turned over all heel flap stitches. Therefore, it is more practical to work all the heel stitches on one needle in order to avoid holes from forming. Work a double-beaded selvage here too.

Arrange the heel stitches on three needles: two equal side panels and one center panel. If the number of stitches is not divisible by three, put the rest of the stitches on the center panel needle. The stitch arrangement for all sizes is given in the chart. The figure between the slashes (/) is the number of stitches of the center panel; the two outer figures are the number of stitches on either side.

Pick up the correct number of stitches along both sides of the heel flap with one of the free double-pointed needles in the correct size.

NUMBER OF STITCHES FOR THE ROUND HEEL WITH FINGERING/4-PLY SOCK YARN
1¾ oz./50g, 230 yards/210m, 30 stitches x 42 rows to 4"/10cm

Children's and women's sizes	5/5½	6/7	8/9	9½/10	11/11½	12/13	1/2	3/4	5/6	7/8	9/9½	10/11	12/13	14/15
Men's sizes										5/6	7/8	9/10	11/12	13/14
Continental sizes	20/21	22/23	24/25	26/27	28/29	30/31	32/33	34/35	36/37	38/39	40/41	42/43	44/45	46/47
Total stitches/ per needle	44/11	44/11	48/12	48/12	52/13	52/13	56/14	56/14	60/15	60/15	64/16	64/16	68/17	72/18
Total stitches per heel	22	22	24	24	26	26	28	28	30	30	32	32	34	36
Heel flap arrangement	7/8/7		8/8/8		8/10/8		9/10/9		10/10/10		10/12/10		11/12/11	12/12/12

NUMBER OF STITCHES FOR THE ROUND HEEL WITH DK/6-PLY SOCK YARN
1¾ oz./50g, 137 yards/125m, 22 stitches x 30 rows = 4"/10cm

Children's and womens sizes	5/5½	6/7	8/9	9½/10	11/11½	12/13	1/2	3/4	5/6	7/8	9/9½	10/11	12/13	14/15
Men's sizes										5/6	7/8	9/10	11/12	13/14
Continental sizes	20/21	22/23	24/25	26/27	28/29	30/31	32/33	34/35	36/37	38/39	40/41	42/43	44/45	46/47
Total stitches/ per needle	32/8	32/8	36/9	36/9	40/10	40/10	44/11	44/11	48/12	48/12	52/13	52/13	52/13	56/14
Total stitches per heel	16	16	18	18	20	20	22	22	24	24	26	26	26	28
Heel flap arrangement	5/6/5		6/6/6		6/8/6		7/8/7		8/8/8		8/10/8			9/10/9

Start at the center of the heel on a right-side row. The side panels are left on the side, each on a separate needle; the center panel has been half worked.

Row 1 (½ right-side row): Work in stockinette stitch, slip the last stitch of the center panel, leave the needle on one side, slip the first stitch of the side panel, knit both stitches together (left slanting). Attach a stitch marker to the right working needle, knit the remaining stitches, turn at the end of the row.

The following rows are easier to work if the stitches from Needles 2 and 3 that had been left on one side are now arranged evenly across two double-pointed needles.

Row 2 (wrong-side row): First knit and then purl the first stitch. Slip the marker from the left-hand to the right-hand needle in the same position. After working the stitches on Needle 1, you are back at the center of the heel. Purl the stitches on Needle 2 (½ center panel), slip the last stitch, leave the needle on one side. Slip the slipped stitch back onto the left-hand needle, purl both stitches together.

Attach a second marker, purl the remaining stitches, turn at the end of the row. Now all the heel stitches are on one double-pointed needle.

Row 3 (right-side row): Knit all the stitches, continue past the front marker, slip the stitch before the next marker, remove the marker, slip the next stitch, knit both stitches together. Slip the marker back onto the right-hand needle, knit the remaining stitches, turn at the end of the row.

Row 4 (wrong-side row): First knit then purl the first stitch, continue past the front marker, slip the stitch before the next marker, remove the marker, slip the slipped stitch back onto the left-hand needle, purl both stitches together with the following stitch. Attach a marker onto the right-hand needle, purl the remaining stitches, and turn at the end of the row.

Repeat rows 3 and 4 until only the stitches of the center panel remain on the needle. If the heel is to be reinforced, add the extra strength either by working in a second yarn or by weaving it in at the end.

PICKING UP STITCHES AND THE GUSSET

Once the heel is turned, continue working in rounds and, at the same time, on the first round, pick up new stitches along the double-beaded selvage on either side of the heel flap (= 1 stitch into each bead).

Work 1 more round over all stitches in rounds for the sole: Work the stitches on Needles 2 and 3 in pattern and those on Needles 1 and 4 in stockinette stitch. Arrange the stitches on Needles 4 and 1 so that there are the same number of stitches on both needles. Then mark the round change between Needles 4 and 1.

To avoid side holes, pick up the horizontal strand between the heel and the upper foot on either side of this round, slip it twisted onto the needle, and knit it together with the outer stitches of the upper foot (= the first stitch on Needle 2 and the last stitch on Needle 3) or with the outer stitches of the heel (= the last stitch on Needle 1 and first stitch on Needle 4).

The decreases worked for the gusset have not yet eliminated all the extra stitches so that you are back to the original number. On the following rounds, the number of stitches for the gusset is gradually reduced back to the original number.

Begin at the start of the round for Needle 1. After picking up the stitches along the side of the heel flap, you have already worked one round.

DECREASE ROUND

Knit all the stitches on Needle 1, work to 3 stitches from the end of Needle 1 and knit the next 2 stitches together (right slanting), knit 1. Work the stitches on Needles 2 and 3 in pattern, knit all the stitches on Needle 4, slipping the second and third stitches and knitting both stitches together (left slanting).

Repeat this decrease round until you have the same number of stitches on the heel needles as you had at the beginning.

Continue in rounds for the foot.

HEELS WITH DIAGONAL SEAMS

Heels with diagonal seams have a small kink at the base of the heel as a result of more rows being worked over the stitches at the center of the heel than over the stitches along the sides. With the exception of the mock short-row heel, in which this effect is achieved by working increases and decreases, all other diagonal seams are formed by working short rows. Without the addition of a gusset—formed by increasing or decreasing—or a heel flap, these heels do not allow the instep much space.

Heels with diagonal seams include:

- the short-row heel
- the short-row heel with reinforced double stitches
- the short-row heel with round shaping
- the wrap stitch heel
- the gusset with increases and decreases
- the hybrid heel
- the mock short-row heel

Tip

Heels with diagonal seams are easy to reinforce by working in a second yarn or by weaving it in at the end. Slipped stitch patterns could also be incorporated, but those very important double-beaded stitches or wrap stitches frequently look uneven and have holes.

Note

Heels with diagonal seams are shorter than heels with heel flaps. If you prefer to make the heel flaps look longer work the stitches on Needles 1 and 4 in stockinette stitch for $1/2$" to $3/4$" before starting the heel, continuing in leg pattern over the stitches on Needles 2 and 3.

SHORT ROWS AND EXTENDED SHORT ROWS

When working short rows, only part of the stitches are worked and then turned in the middle of a row. The remaining stitches are left on one side until later. When you later continue over those stitches that were left on one side, you will frequently find that there are small holes at the original stopping points. Avoid these holes wherever possible, especially on the toes and heels, which are subject to increased wear and tear. To avoid holes from forming, work the last stitch of a short row, also known as the turning stitch, as a double stitch or wrap stitch. Make sure that the stranded yarn is pulled up firmly.

For a simple short row, the turning stitch marks the new end of the row. It will not be worked on the following rows. If several short rows are worked one above the other, each time you reach the end of a short row, work another regular stitch as a turning stitch and leave it on one side. For the upper part of the heel, shorten the number of stitches on every row over the stitches on Needles 4 and 1. Therefore, on either side of the heel stitches, the number of turning stitches increases from the outside to the inside from row to row, and increasingly fewer stitches are worked regularly at the center.

For extended short rows, the turning stitch marks the end of the row as well. To extend a row, work 1 additional stitch at the end of the row. Work a new turning stitch into this stitch, thereby moving the end of the row by 1 stitch to the outside, and continue to extend this on the following rows as well.

On the lower part of the heel with diagonal seams, the regularly worked stitches increase from the center of the heel to either side on every row.

From a technical standpoint, knitting socks with short rows is a good idea if you have trouble picking up stitches evenly along a beaded selvage. On the other hand, double stitches and wrap stitches have to be worked very carefully and cannot be too loose. Beginning knitters tend to work too tightly, so they should be able to work short rows very well. The more you knit and the quicker you become, however, the looser your hands and the stitches can become, so you may need to use slightly smaller needles.

OTHER USES FOR HEELS WITH DIAGONAL SEAMS

Heels with diagonal seams have a great advantage: they can also be used for the toe shaping. Particularly suited to this are heels with reinforced seam stitches, the wrap stitch heel, the mock short-row heel, and the short-row heel with reinforced double stitches. They have no holes and can withstand hard wear (see page 77, "Diagonal Seam Heel for Toes").

With the exception of the short-row heel with round shaping, all heels with diagonal seams can be worked toe-up. Socks are described as toe-up when they are not worked from the cuff down, as has been done so far, but rather are worked upward, starting with the toes (see page 81, "Socks Knit from the Toe Up"). The heels are then upside down, but still provide a good fit.

Short-row heel as a toe

Short-Row Heel

Heel with short rows and double stitches
. . . narrow heel, low instep

This short-row heel is the standard heel with diagonal seams. The double stitches have to be worked very carefully, and the yarn tension must be very even; otherwise there will be holes. The two rounds that are worked over all the stitches between the upper and lower sections may break up some leg patterns.

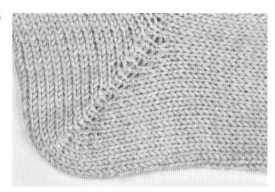

continue on pages 54 and 55

LESSON: Working Double Stitches

Work the last stitch of a short row as for all remaining stitches, then turn the work. Hold the yarn at the front of the work and slip the stitch as if to purl. If you now pull the yarn firmly to the back, this will bring both loops of the lower stitch over the needle, forming a double stitch. The yarn is now at the back of the work. To continue to purl, bring the yarn to the front of the work between the needles.

Note

Remember that double stitches left on one side form the end of the rows.

Double stitches on right-side rows

Work the last stitch, turn.

Bring the yarn to the front of the work, slip the stitch.

Pull the yarn firmly to the back.

Completed double stitch

Double stitches on wrong-side rows

Work the last stitch, turn.

Bring the yarn to the front of the work, slip the stitch.

Pull the yarn firmly to the back.

Completed double stitch

WORKING DOUBLE STITCHES

Work the double stitches as for 1 stitch.
Make sure you pick up both loops and work them off together.

Knitwise

Purlwise

53

NUMBER OF STITCHES FOR HEELS WITH DIAGONAL SEAMS WITH FINGERING/4-PLY SOCK YARN

1³/₄ oz./50g, 230 yards/210m, 30 stitches x 42 rows to 4"/10cm

Children's and women's sizes	5/5½	6/7	8/9	9½/10	11/11½	12/13	1/2	3/4	5/6	7/8	9/9½	10/11	12/13	14/15
Men's sizes										5/6	7/8	9/10	11/12	13/14
Continenatal sizes	20/21	22/23	24/25	26/27	28/29	30/31	32/33	34/35	36/37	38/39	40/41	42/43	44/45	46/47
Total stitches/ per needle	44/11	44/11	48/12	48/12	52/13	52/13	56/14	56/14	60/15	60/15	64/16	64/16	68/17	72/18
Heel flap arrangment	7/8/7		8/8/8		8/10/8		9/10/9		10/10/10		10/12/10		11/12/11	12/12/12

NUMBER OF STITCHES FOR HEELS WITH DIAGONAL SEAMS WITH DK/6-PLY SOCK YARN

1³/₄ oz./50g, 137 yards/125m, 22 stitches x 30 rows to 4"/10cm

Children's and women's sizes	5/5½	6/7	8/9	9½/10	11/11½	12/13	1/2	3/4	5/6	7/8	9/9½	10/11	12/13	14/15
Men's sizes										5/6	7/8	9/10	11/12	13/14
Continental sizes	20/21	22/23	24/25	26/27	28/29	30/31	32/33	34/35	36/37	38/39	40/41	42/43	44/45	46/47
Total stitches/ per needle	32/8	32/8	36/9	36/9	40/10	40/10	44/11	44/11	48/12	48/12	52/13	52/13	52/13	56/14
Heel flap arrangement	5/6/5		6/6/6		6/8/6		7/8/7		8/8/8		8/10/8			9/10/9

In your mind, arrange the heel stitches so that you have two equal side panels and one center panel. The stitch arrangement for all sizes is given in the charts above. The figure between the two slashes (//) applies to the center panel; the two outer figures are the number of stitches on either side.

UPPER SECTION

Slip the stitches on Needles 2 and 3 onto a stitch holder. Dependent on the space needed for knitting, it is easier to leave the stitches on Needles 1 and 4 on their needles, slip them onto one needle, or arrange them on three needles as indicated in the chart. Start the heel at the center of a right-side row between Needles 4 and 1.

Work the last stitch of every row as a double stitch so that there is 1 double stitch more at the end of every row of the heel. The rows get shorter, and fewer and fewer stitches are worked on every row.

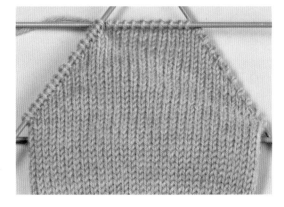

Row 1 (¹/₂ right-side row): Knit all the stitches, working 1 double stitch into the last stitch.

Row 2 (wrong-side row): Bring the yarn to the front between the two needles, purl all the stitches, work 1 double stitch into the last stitch.

Row 3 (right-side row): Knit all the stitches, work 1 double stitch into the last stitch before the double stitch at the end of the row. Make sure you have not skipped any stitches, because the last regular stitch and the double stitch are frequently very close together.

Row 4 (wrong-side row): Bring the yarn to the front between the two needles, purl all the stitches, work 1 double stitch into the last stitch.

Repeat rows 3 and 4 until all the stitches of the side panels are worked as double stitches. The stitches of the center panel still appear as regular stitches.

ADDITIONAL ROUNDS

When all the double stitches have been worked for the upper section, work 2 additional rounds over all the stitches and double stitches on all four needles. At the same time, work the stitches on Needles 1 and 4 in stockinette stitch

LOWER SECTION

When the 2 additional rounds are complete, work extended short rows (see page 52, "Short Rows and Extended Short Rows") with double stitches. Unlike the upper section, start with the inner side stitches, and on every row work 1 more stitch over the double stitch of the previous row.

Row 1 (right-side row): Knit all the stitches of the center panel, work 1 double stitch into the next stitch (= the first stitch of the side panel).

Row 2 (wrong-side row): Purl all the stitches, then work 1 double stitch into the next stitch.

Row 3 (right-side row): Knit all the stitches up to the double stitch of the previous row, knit the double stitch and then knit 1 more stitch. Work 1 double stitch into this last stitch.

Row 4 (wrong-side row): Purl all the stitches up to the double stitch of the previous row, purl the double stitch and then purl 1 more stitch. Work 1 double stitch into this last stitch.

To get the stitch arrangement shown in the chart above, you must work your stitches off three needles. If the heel stitches are arranged only on one or two needles, this trapezoid shape will not appear until later.

and those on Needles 2 and 3 in the leg pattern. When inserting the needle into the double stitches, make sure you pick up both loops. Then leave the stitches on Needles 2 and 3 on one side again.

Repeat rows 3 and 4 until the two outer heel stitches appear on the needle as double stitches. End with half of a right-side row at the center of the heel between the stitches on Needles 4 and 1.

Continue in rounds with a second double-pointed needle, working all stitches back on their original needles. At the same time, knit the last double stitch on Needle 1 and the first double stitch on Needle 4.

To avoid side holes, pick up the horizontal strand between the heel and the upper foot on either side on the first round after finishing the heel, slip it twisted onto the needle, and knit it together with the outer stitches of the upper foot (= the first stitch on Needle 2 and the last stitch on Needle 3) or with the outer stitches of the heel (= the last stitch on Needle 1 and the first stitch on Needle 4).

Continue in rounds for the foot.

Tip

To avoid side holes, pick up the horizontal strand between the heel and the upper foot on either side on the first round after finishing the heel, slip it twisted onto the needle, and knit it together with the outer stitches of the upper foot (= the first stitch on Needle 2 and the last stitch on Needle 3) or with the outer stitches of the heel (= the last stitch on Needle 1 and the first stitch on Needle 4).

continue on page 73

Short-Row Heel with Reinforced Double Stitches

. . . narrow heel, low instep

Reinforced double stitches create a stronger side seam that is less susceptible to wear-and-tear. No additional rounds are needed over all the stitches between the upper and lower panels as there are for some leg patterns. However, the double stitches have to be worked very carefully, and the yarn tension must be very even; otherwise there will be holes.

The upper and lower sections of this heel are worked the same as for the standard short-row heel. However, since the additional rounds are omitted for short-row heels worked with reinforced double stitches, you work a double stitch—the reinforced double stitch—into a double stitch of the previous row of the lower section.

Leave the stitches on Needles 2 and 3 on one side.

Start the heel at the center of a right-side row between Needles 4 and 1.

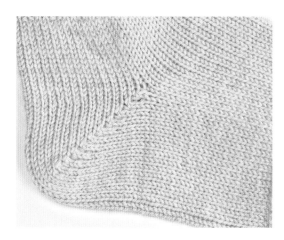

UPPER SECTION

This section is worked the same as for the upper section of the short-row heel. The arrangement of the stitches (heel and side panels) is the same as for the short-row heel. For more information on the number and arrangement of the stitches, see the charts on page 54, "Number of Stitches for Heels with Diagonal Seams."

Row 1 ($^1/_2$ right-side row): Knit all the stitches, working 1 double stitch into the last stitch.

Row 2 (wrong-side row): Bring the yarn to the front between the two needles, purl all the stitches, work 1 double stitch into the last stitch.

Row 3 (right-side row): Knit all the stitches, work 1 double stitch into the last stitch before the double stitch at the end of the row. Make sure that you have not skipped any stitches, because the last regular stitch and the double stitch are frequently very close together.

Row 4 (wrong-side row): Bring the yarn to the front between the two needles, purl all the stitches, work 1 double stitch into the last stitch.

Repeat rows 3 and 4 until all the stitches of the side panels have been worked as double stitches. The stitches of the center panel still appear as regular stitches.

LOWER SECTION

When the upper section is complete, continue with the short-row heel for the lower section without working any additional rounds.

Row 1 (right-side row): Knit all the stitches of the center panel, work 1 new reinforced double stitch into the first double stitch: work 1 double stitch, turn, bring the yarn to the front of the work and pull it firmly to the back and pull. There are now 4 threads on the needle for the reinforced double stitch.

Row 2 (wrong-side row): Purl all the stitches, work 1 new, reinforced double stitch into the next double stitch.

Row 3 (right-side row): Knit all the stitches and the next reinforced double stitch, work 1 reinforced double stitch into the next double stitch.

Row 4 (wrong-side row): Purl all the stitches and the next reinforced double stitch, work 1 reinforced double stitch into the next double stitch.

When working the reinforced double stitches, make sure you pick up both loops. The reinforced double stitches only look bulky when you are working them. They are not obvious in the sock itself.

Repeat rows 3 and 4 until the last heel stitch on Needle 1 and the first heel stitch on Needle 4 appear as reinforced double stitches on the needle. End with half of a right-side row at the center of the heel between the stitches on Needles 4 and 1.

Continue in rounds with a second double-pointed needle, working all the stitches back on their original needle. At the same time, knit the last reinforced double stitch on Needle 1 and the first reinforced double stitch on Needle 4.

Continue in rounds for the foot.

Short-Row Heel with Round Shaping

... wide heel, low instep

The short-row heel with round shaping is an attractive variation for wide heels. The double stitches have to be worked very carefully, and the yarn tension must be very even; otherwise there will be holes. The two rounds that are worked over all the stitches between the upper and lower sections may break up some leg patterns.

For the short-row heel with round shaping, work the upper section of the standard short-row heel with 2 additional rounds.

Leave the stitches on Needles 2 and 3 on one side.

Start the heel at the center of a right-side row between Needles 1 and 4.

The heel is now worked over the stitches on Needles 1 and 4 using short-rows with double stitches.

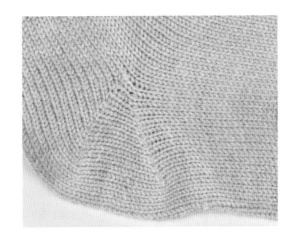

Note

The short-row heel with round shaping is the only heel with diagonal seams that cannot be used for toes as well.

UPPER SECTION

This section is worked the same as for the upper section of the short-row heel. The arrangement of the stitches (heel and side panels) are the same as for the short-row heel. For the number and arrangement of the stitches, see the chart on page 54, "Number of Stitches for Heels with Diagonal Seams."

Row 1 (1/2 right-side row): Knit all the stitches, work 1 double stitch into the last stitch.

Row 2 (wrong-side row): Bring the yarn to the front between the two needles, purl all the stitches work 1 double stitch into the last stitch.

Row 3 (right-side row): Knit all the stitches, work 1 double stitch into the last stitch before the double stitch at the end of the row. Make sure that you have not skipped any stitches, because the last regular stitch and the double stitch are frequently very close together.

Row 4 (wrong-side row): Bring the yarn to the front between the two needles, purl all the stitches, work 1 double stitch into the last stitch.

Repeat rows 3 and 4 until all the stitches of the side panels have been worked as double stitches. The stitches of the center panel still appear as regular stitches.

ADDITIONAL ROUNDS

When all the double stitches have been worked for the upper section, work 2 additional rounds over all the stitches and double stitches on all 4 needles. At the same time, work the stitches on Needles 1 and 4 in stockinette stitch, and those on Needles 2 and 3 in leg pattern. When inserting the needle into the double stitches, make sure you pick up both loops. Then leave the stitches on Needles 2 and 3 on one side again.

LOWER SECTION

For the lower section, work the same as for the upper section. End with half of a right-side row at the center of the heel between the stitches on Needles 4 and 1.

Continue in rounds with a second double-pointed needle, working all the stitches back on their original needles. At the same time, knit the last double stitch on Needle 1 and the first double stitch on Needle 4.

To avoid side holes, pick up the horizontal strand between the heel and upper foot on either side on the first round after finishing the heel, slip it twisted onto the needle, and knit it together with the outer stitches of the upper foot (= the first stitch on Needle 2 and the last stitch on Needle 3) or with the outer stitches of the heel (= the last stitch on Needle 1 and the first stitch on Needle 4).

Continue in rounds for the foot.

Wrap Stitch Heel

... narrow heel, low instep

The wrap stitch heel has a stronger side seam that is less susceptible to holes. There are no additional rounds to break up some leg patterns.

Small straight strands of yarn make the wrap stitch seam very visible.

Start the heel at the center of a right-side row between Needles 4 and 1.

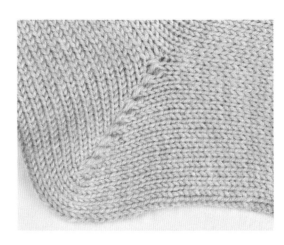

UPPER SECTION

The arrangement of the stitches of the side panels and the center panel is the same as for the short-row heel. For the number and arrangement of the stitches, see the charts on page 54, "Number of Stitches for Heels with Diagonal Seams."

Row 1 (right-side row): Knit all the stitches except the last one, work the last stitch as a wrap stitch.

Row 2 (wrong-side row): Purl all the stitches except the last one, work the last stitch as a wrap stitch.

Row 3 (right-side row): Bring the yarn between the needles to the back of the work, knit all the stitches except the last one, work the last stitch as a wrap stitch.

Row 4 (wrong-side row): Purl all the stitches except the last stitch before the wrap stitch, work the last stitch as a wrap stitch.

Repeat rows 3 and 4 until all the stitches of the side panels have been worked as wrap stitches. The stitches of the center panel still appear as regular stitches.

Note

Unlike the double stitch, the stitch that forms the wrap stitch is no longer worked. Completed wrap stitches are stitches that have been left on one side. They form the end of the row of short rows.

LESSON: Working Wrap Stitches

Bring the yarn to the front of the work, slip the stitch to be wrapped purlwise onto the right-hand needle, turn the work, leave the working yarn in your left hand and bring the yarn around the stitch. Slip the first stitch and pull up the yarn firmly.

Leave the stitches on Needles 2 and 3 on one side.

Work the heel over the stitches on Needles 4 and 1 with simple short rows with wrap stitches on either side.

Yarn at the front of the work

Slip stitch purlwise.

Turn, yarn in the left hand.

WORKING WRAP STITCHES

If you have to work a wrap stitch, first slip this unworked stitch onto the right-hand needle regardless of whether it is a single or a double wrap stitch on the front or back of the work

Working wrap stitches on the first right-side row

Pick up the wrap yarn with the left-hand needle.

Slip the wrap yarn onto the right-hand needle.

Knit the stitch and wrap the yarn together.

Working wrap stitches on the first wrong-side row

Pick up the wrap yarn with the left-hand needle.

Slip the wrap yarn onto the right-hand needle.

Purl the stitch and wrap the yarn together.

Working wrap stitches on all other right-side rows

Pick up the wrap yarns with the left-hand needle.

Slip the wrap yarns onto the right-hand needle.

Knit the stitch and wrap the yarns together.

Working wrap stitches on all other wrong-side rows

Pick up the wrap yarns with the left-hand needle.

Slip the wrap yarns onto the right-hand needle.

Purl the stitch and wrap the yarns together.

LOWER SECTION

The lower section is joined to the wrap stitch heel without any additional rows.

Row 1 (right-side row): Knit, slip the first wrap stitch, pick up the wrap yarn with the left-hand needle, slip it onto the right-hand needle, and knit both stitches: insert the left-hand needle into both stitches from the left so that the left-hand needle is in front of the right-hand needle and bring the working yarn through both stitches. Work a wrap stitch into the next stitch (= this stitch has now been wrapped twice).

Row 2 (wrong-side row): Purl, slip the first wrap stitch, slip the wrap yarn onto the left-hand needle and purl it together with the stitch. Work a wrap stitch into the next stitch (= this stitch has now been wrapped twice).

Row 3 (right-side row): Knit, slip the next wrap stitch, slip the 2 wrap yarns onto the left-hand needle and knit them both together with the stitch. Wrap the next stitch again, turn.

Row 4 (wrong-side row): Purl, slip the next wrap stitch, slip the 2 wrap yarns onto the left-hand needle and purl them both together with the stitch. Wrap the next stitch again, turn.

Repeat rows 3 and 4 until the 2 outer heel stitches on the needle are wrap stitches. End with half of a right-side row at the center of the heel between the stitches on Needles 4 and 1. Continue in rounds with a second double-pointed needle, working all the stitches back on their original needles. At the same time, knit the last wrap stitch on Needle 1 and the first wrap stitch on Needle 4.

Continue in rounds for the foot.

Gusset with Increases and Decreases
. . . narrow foot, high instep

The gusset gives the heel with diagonal seams considerably more space both in the heel and in the instep, and it can be widened by the addition of extra stitches. All heels worked using short rows as well as the mock short-row heel can be widened in this way.

Start the heel on a right-side row between Needles 1 and 4. Start working the gusset decreases when the number of rows that still have to be worked for the leg is two times the number of stitches that still have to be picked up for the gusset (see the following chart).

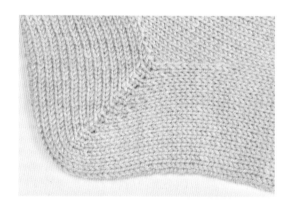

NUMBER OF STITCHES TO BE PICKED UP FOR THE GUSSET WITH FINGERING/4-PLY SOCK YARN
1¾ oz./50g, 230 yards/210m, 30 stitches x 42 rows = 4"/10cm

Children's and womens sizes	5/5½	6/7	8/9	9½/10	11/11½	12/13	1/2	3/4	5/6	7/8	9/9½	10/11	12/13	14/15
Men's sizes										5/6	7/8	9/10	11/12	13/14
Continental sizes	20/21	22/23	24/25	26/27	28/29	30/31	32/33	34/35	36/37	38/39	40/41	42/43	44/45	46/47
Total stitches/per needle	44/11	44/11	48/12	48/12	52/13	52/13	56/14	56/14	60/15	60/15	64/16	64/16	68/17	72/18
Heel flap arrangement	7/8/7		8/8/8		8/10/8		9/10/9		10/10/10		10/12/10		11/12/11	12/12/12
Total stitches per gusset	4		4		4		5		5		5		6	6

NUMBER OF STITCHES TO BE PICKED UP FOR THE GUSSET WITH DK/6-PLY SOCK YARN

1¾ oz./50g, 137 yards/125m, 22 stitches x 30 rows = 4"/10cm

Children's and women's sizes	5/5½	6/7	8/9	9½/10	11/11½	12/13	1/2	3/4	5/6	7/8	9/9½	10/11	12/13	14/15
Men's sizes										5/6	7/8	9/10	11/12	13/14
Continental sizes	20/21	22/23	24/25	26/27	28/29	30/31	32/33	34/35	36/37	38/39	40/41	42/43	44/45	46/47
Total stitches / per needle	32/8	32/8	36/9	36/9	40/10	40/10	44/11	44/11	48/12	48/12	52/13	52/13	52/13	56/14
Heel flap arrangement	5/6/5		6/6/6		6/8/6		7/8/7		8/8/8		8/10/8			9/10/9
Total stitches per gusset	3		3		3		4		4		4			5

INCREASING GUSSET STITCHES

Increase round: pick up and make 1 stitch knitwise through the back of the horizontal strand between Needles 1 and 2 and between Needles 3 and 4. (To make 1 stitch, insert the left-hand needle under the horizontal strand between two stitches from front to back, and knit the picked up strand through the back loop.)

These new stitches are part of the stitches of the upper foot and should be on Needles 2 and 3. Continue over these stitches in leg pattern, or alternately, if you prefer the heel to start higher visually, the stitches on Needles 4 and 1 in sto-ckinette stitch. Repeat the increase round on every second round until you reach the number of gusset stitches desired.

HEEL WITH DIAGONAL SEAMS

Leave the stitches on Needles 2 and 3 on one side.
Now work the heel with a diagonal seam over the stit-ches on Needles 4 and 1.

This is suitable for all heels with a diagonal seam with the exception of the hybrid heel, because that form of heel already has a gusset.

DECREASING GUSSET STITCHES

Gusset decreases continue on after the last row of the heel, working short rows.
Decrease round: slip the last stitch on Needle 1 and the first stitch on Needle 2, and knit both stitches together (left slanting), work the stitches on Needles 2 and 3 in pattern, knit the last stitch on Needle 3 and the first stitch on Needle 4 together (right slanting).

The following decrease rounds are easier to manage if the outer heel stitches (= the first stitch on Needle 4 and the last stitch on Needle 1) are slipped onto Needles 2 and 3 and not slipped back again until the end of the gusset. Repeat these decrease rounds on every second round until all additional gusset stitches have been decreased and you have the original number of stitches on the needles again.
Continue in rounds for the foot.

Hybrid Heel
. . . narrow heel, high instep

The hybrid heel is a combination of a short-row heel and a short heel flap with a gusset. It gives much more room in the heel and instep and can also be widened even more by adding heel flap rows if needed.

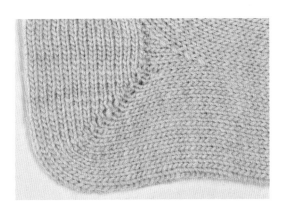

Note

Sometimes it is easier to work a new stitch into the last stitch than it is to pick up a new stitch from the horizontal strand. To do this, first work the last stitch before the increase in stockinette stitch and then work it again through the back of the loop.

NUMBER OF STITCHES TO BE PICKED UP FOR THE GUSSET WITH FINGERING/4-PLY SOCK YARN

1¾ oz./50g, 230 yards/210m, 30 stitches x 42 rows = 4"/10cm

Children's and women's sizes	5/5½	6/7	8/9	9½/10	11/11½	12/13	1/2	3/4	5/6	7/8	9/9½	10/11	12/13	14/15
Men's sizes										5/6	7/8	9/10	11/12	13/14
Continental sizes	20/21	22/23	24/25	26/27	28/29	30/31	32/33	34/35	36/37	38/39	40/41	42/43	44/45	46/47
Total stitches/ per needle	44/11	44/11	48/12	48/12	52/13	52/13	56/14	56/14	60/15	60/15	64/16	64/16	68/17	72/18
Heel flap arrangement	7/8/7		8/8/8		8/10/8		9/10/9		10/10/10		10/12/10		11/12/11	12/12/12
Total stitches per gusset	4		4		4		5		5		5		6	6
Heel flap/rows	8						10						12	

NUMBER OF STITCHES TO BE PICKED UP FOR THE GUSSET WITH DK/6-PLY SOCK YARN

1¾ oz./50g, 137 yards/125m, 22 stitches x 30 rows = 4"/10cm

Children's and women's sizes	5/5½	6/7	8/9	9½/10	11/11½	12/13	1/2	3/4	5/6	7/8	9/9½	10/11	12/13	14/15
Men's sizes,										5/6	7/8	9/10	11/12	13/14
Continental sizes	20/21	22/23	24/25	26/27	28/29	30/31	32/33	34/35	36/37	38/39	40/41	42/43	44/45	46/47
Total stitches/ per needle	32/8	32/8	36/9	36/9	40/10	40/10	44/11	44/11	48/12	48/12	52/13	52/13	52/13	56/14
Heel flap arrangement	5/6/5		6/6/6		6/8/6		7/8/7		8/8/8		8/10/8			9/10/9
Total stitches per gusset	3		3		3		4		4		4			5
Heel flap/rows	6						8							10

HEEL FLAP

Leave the stitches on Needles 2 and 3 on one side.
   Continue over the stitches on Needles 4 and 1, working a short heel flap in open rows, knit the 2 selvage stitches on every row, forming a double-beaded selvage. The heel flap has the right height when the number of beads on either side is the same as the number of gusset stitches required (see chart above).

HEELS WITH DIAGONAL SEAMS

Apart from the heel with diagonal seams with increases and decreases (see page 60), all the other heels with diagonal seams are suitable to be worked as hybrid heels. For the heel variations with additional rows, start to pick up the new stitches along the side edges of the heel flap on the first additional round, and continue picking up stitches when the heel is completed.
   For the heel variations without additional rows, start to pick up the additional stitches and working gusset decreases right after the foot is completed.

PICKING UP STITCHES WITH GUSSET DECREASES

In order to continue working the foot in rounds, you will need to pick up new stitches along the double-beaded selvage on either side of the heel flap (= 1 stitch into each bead). Work 1 more round over all the needles for the sole: work the stitches on Needles 2 and 3 in pattern and those on Needles 4 and 1 in stockinette stitch.
   The extra stitches on Needles 4 and 1 will be eliminated by the gusset decreases after another round.

DECREASE ROUND

Knit all the stitches on Needle 1, work to 3 stitches from the end of Needle 1 and knit the next 2 stitches together (right slanting), knit 1. Work the stitches on Needles 2 and 3 in pattern, knit all the stitches on Needle 4, slipping the second and third stitches and knitting both stitches together (left slanting).
   Repeat this decrease round every second round until you have the same number of stitches on the needles as you had at the beginning.
   Continue in rounds for the foot.

Mock Short-Row Heel

... narrow heel, low instep

The mock short-row heel isn't formed by short rows, but rather by decreases and increases along the beaded edge. It's a good alternative for anyone who is looking for a short-row fit but has trouble working short rows.

Start this heel on a right-side row between Needles 1 and 4.

Leave the stitches on Needles 2 and 3 on one side.

Now work the heel over the stitches on Needles 4 and 1 in flat stockinette stitch. Make sure the beaded edge is kept neat (= knit the first and last stitch on every row).

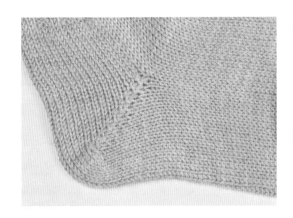

Tip

The mock short-row heel usually looks neater than the other heels with diagonal side seams, and does not have holes.

UPPER SECTION

The arrangement of the stitches of the side panels and the center panel is the same as for the short-row heel. For the number and arrangement of the stitches, see the charts on page 54, "Number of Stitches for Heels with Diagonal Seams."

Row 1 ($\frac{1}{2}$ right-side row): Knit all the stitches, knit the last 2 stitches together.

Row 2 (wrong-side row): Knit the first stitch, purl all the stitches except the last 2 stitches on the needle, knit both stitches together, forming a bead at the end.

Row 3 (right-side row): Knit all the stitches except the last 2 stitches on the needle, then knit both stitches together.

Repeat rows 2 and 3 until only the stitches of the center panel between the beaded edges remain on the needle. End with a wrong-side row over all stitches.

Upper section of the mock short-row heel

TURNING ROWS

Work another 2 rows over all the stitches without any decreases.

Right-side row: Slip the first stitch, knit all the remaining stitches.

Wrong-side row: Slip 1 stitch, purl all the remaining stitches (including the last stitch).

LOWER SECTION

Row 1 (right-side row): Slip 1 stitch, knit all the stitches, at the end of the row knit 1 more stitch into the next bead, turn.

Row 2 (wrong-side row): Slip 1 stitch, purl all the stitches, at the end of the row purl 1 more stitch into the next bead, turn.

Repeat rows 1 and 2 until a new stitch has been picked up into each bead.

End with half of a right-side row at the center of the heel between the stitches on Needles 4 and 1. Continue in rounds with a second double-pointed needle.

Continue in rounds for the foot.

ROUND HEELS JOINED AT THE FOOT

If you like knitting in rounds or think your stitches are too irregular when you are working open rows, then these socks are an ideal alternative because they are worked entirely without wrong-side rows (and therefore without any purl stitches), and can be made to fit any heel according to the way you form the gusset.

Round heels include:

- the plain heel
- the peasant heel
- the "afterthought" heel with waste yarn

Tip

After the gusset decreases, advanced knitters can have fun by working an attractive toe shaping following the instructions for a heel. All rounded toes can be adapted and personalized by working either a larger or smaller gusset.

The plain heel is worked from the leg right into the sock. Cast on new stitches at the point where the heel starts using the waste yarn. These stitches replace the stitches on Needles 2 and 3. If more stitches need to be cast on than were originally on the needles, then half a gusset can be worked over the following rows. The second half of the gusset will later be on the opposite side of the new cast-on stitches.

Continue in rounds over the stitches on Needles 1 and 4, as well as the new cast-on stitches on Needles 2* and 3*, working a heel that runs down to the lower end of the heel. The heel ends where the foot touches the floor, and there are many ways of continuing: by working a double decrease (this needs fewer purl stitches), by working Kitchener stitch, or by decreasing and pulling together the last stitches.

When the heel is complete, pick up the stitches along the loop cast-on. These stitches replace the stitches on Needles 4 and 1. This way you can continue working the foot in rounds.

The **"afterthought" heel,** which includes the peasant heel, is also worked in rounds and closed at the sole. The advantage of this is that you can work complicated patterns in one piece from the cuff right down to the toes (or vice versa), without having to go through the heel. The motifs, patterns, and stripes of self-patterning yarns are not interrupted. If constant wear in firm shoes should result in a heel getting thin, this is easily removed and knitted back in.

To work an "afterthought" heel, arrange the stitches on Needles 4 and 1 at the height of the heel so that new stitches can later be picked up. This can be done by inserting a contrasting yarn (Peasant Heel), or by leaving stitches on a holder, and at the same time casting on new stitches using an auxiliary yarn.

When the sock is finished, slip all heel stitches onto four double-pointed needles and work the heel decreases as well as finishing the heel.

Tips on Working Round Heels

Round heels can be closed in various ways at the lower end of the heel. Working either Kitchener stitch or double decreases makes for a slightly wider heel. If you pull the last 8 stitches together, this will create a nice rounded shape.

CLOSING THE HEEL BY PULLING STITCHES TOGETHER

Continue the decrease round of the heel decreases on every round until just 2 stitches remain on each needle. Cut the working yarn and weave it through the stitches with a blunt darning needle in the direction of the knitting. Pick up each stitch individually with the darning needle, pull the stitch up. Then pull the yarn through. Pull up carefully and darn the yarn away on the inside. When all the stitches have been darned away this way, the result is firm and hole-free.

Pulling the last 8 stitches together to form a ring

CLOSING THE HEEL USING KITCHENER STITCH

Transition Round

Knit all the stitches on Needles 1 and 3 except the last stitch on Needle 1 and the first stitch on Needle 3, knit both stitches together (right slanting); slip the last stitch on Needle 2 and the first stitch on Needle 4, knit both stitches together (left slanting).

These transition rounds solve the problem of "ears." Then knit across Needle 1 once more to the side edge. Hold the two rows of stitches to be joined one behind the other. Cut the working yarn about 24"/60cm long, thread it onto a darning needle, and join the rows of stitches using Kitchener stitch.

Preparing the First Two Stitches

With the darning needle, pick up the first front stitch as if to purl, leaving the stitch on the needle.

With the darning needle, pick up the first back stitch as if to knit, leaving the stitch on the needle.

Kitchener Stitch (see page 15)

Step 1

Insert the darning needle into the front of the stitch as if to knit and darn off, slip the stitch (= right off).

Step 2

Insert the darning needle into the front of the stitch as if to purl and darn off, leave the stitch on the needle (= left).

Step 3

Insert the darning needle through the back of the stitch as if to purl and darn off, slip the stitch (= left off).

Step 4

Insert the darning needle through the back of the stitch as if to knit and darn off, leave the stitch on the needle (= right).

Repeat steps 1 to 4 until all stitches have been darned off.

Work the last 2 stitches without additional stitches and slip off the needle. Pull up the yarn slightly after each step. Always hold the working yarn below the knitting needles.

> The mantra for grafting or working duplicate stitch is:
> **right off, left** front; **left off, right** back.

Closing the Heel Using a Double-Decrease Band

The double-decrease band is worked similar to the gusset of the plain heel, with half a narrow gusset on either side. The stitches of both half gussets meet at the lower point of the heel and can be closed either by using Kitchener stitch or by pulling the stitches together.

Half-Double Decrease

Knit all the stitches on Needle 1.

Knit the first stitch on Needle 2, slip the next 2 stitches, knit both stitches together for a left slant, turn.

Work a gusset back and forth on either side of the 4 stitches of the side band until just the 2 band stitches remain on Needles 1 and 2.

Row 1 (wrong-side row): Slip 1 stitch, purl 2 stitches, purl 2 stitches together.

Row 2 (right-side row): Slip 1 stitch, knit 2 stitches, slip 2 stitches, knit these stitches together.

Repeat these two rows until just the 4 band stitches remain on Needles 1 and 2.

Work this half-double decrease band once more over the stitches on Needles 3 and 4 until the 8 stitches of both side bands meet. Join these stitches either by using Kitchener stitch or by pulling the stitches together with the working yarn.

Double-decrease bands meeting

Note

Two additional double-pointed needles are needed to work the plain heel.

Tip

Advanced knitters can develop other toe-shaping patterns by following the directions for the heel and then modifying them to get a better fit.

Plain Heel

. . . wide heel, high instep

This heel can be worked entirely in rounds, working just knit stitches. The gusset gives the heel a perfect fit.

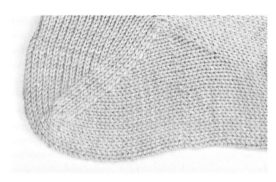

NUMBER OF STITCHES TO BE PICKED UP FOR THE GUSSET WITH FINGERING/4-PLY SOCK YARN

1¾ oz./50g, 230 yards/210m, 30 stitches x 42 rows = 4"/10cm

Children's and women's sizes	5/5½	6/7	8/9	9½/10	11/11½	12/13	1/2	3/4	5/6	7/8	9/9½	10/11	12/13	14/15
Men's sizes										5/6	7/8	9/10	11/12	13/14
Continental sizes	20/21	22/23	24/25	26/27	28/29	30/31	32/33	34/35	36/37	38/39	40/41	42/43	44/45	46/47
Total stitches/ per needle	44/11	44/11	48/12	48/12	52/13	52/13	56/14	56/14	60/15	60/15	64/16	64/16	68/17	72/18
Total stitches per gusset	4		4		4		5		5		5		6	6
Total stitches per needle 2*+ 3*	15		16		17		19		20		21		23	24
To close heel, stitches per needle	6						7						8	

NUMBER OF STITCHES TO BE PICKED UP FOR THE GUSSET WITH DK/6-PLY SOCK YARN

1¾ oz./50g, 137 yards/125m, 22 stitches x 30 rows = 4"/10cm

Children's and women's sizes	5/5½	6/7	8/9	9½/10	11/11½	12/13	1/2	3/4	5/6	7/8	9/9½	10/11	12/13	14/15
Men's sizes										5/6	7/8	9/10	11/12	13/14
Continental sizes	20/21	22/23	24/25	26/27	28/29	30/31	32/33	34/35	36/37	38/39	40/41	42/43	44/45	46/47
Total stitches/ per needle	32/8	32/8	36/9	36/9	40/10	40/10	44/11	44/11	48/12	48/12	52/13	52/13	52/13	56/14
Total stitches per gusset	3		3		3		4		4		4			5
Total stitches per needle 2*+ 3*	11		12		13		15		16		47		17	19
To close heel, stitches per needle	3						4						5	

Start the heel on a right-side row between Needles 4 and 1. Leave the stitches on Needles 2 and 3 on one side. It is easier and clearer to work this heel if the stitches on Needles 2 and 3 are left on the flexible center cable of a circular needle.

PICKING UP STITCHES

Round 1: knit all the stitches on Needle 1, then cast on the correct number of stitches for one needle onto each of the following 2 needles (= Needles 2* and 3*) plus the appropriate number of gusset stitches using the loop cast-on method (see page 27). Knit across Needle 4.

Knit 1 more round over all the stitches.

Alternately, cast on the stitches using the invisible cast-on method (see page 27). This will hide the join.

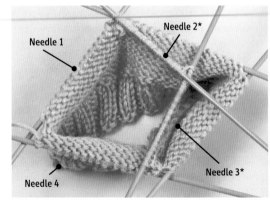

Picking up stitches using the loop cast-on method

DECREASE ROUND

Knit all the stitches; slip the second and third stitches on Needle 2* and knit both stitches together (left slanting). Work to 3 stitches from the end of Needle 3* and knit the next 2 stitches together (right slanting), knit 1. Repeat these decreases on every second round until all the extra gusset stitches have been eliminated.

Knit 1 more round over all stitches, then continue with the heel decreases.

HEEL DECREASES AND CLOSING THE HEEL

Decrease round: knit all the stitches, work to 3 stitches from the end of Needles 1 and 3*, knit the next 2 stitches together (right slanting), knit 1. Slip the second and third stitches on Needles 2* and 4, knit both stitches together (left slanting).

Repeat these decreases on every second round until just the number of stitches remain as are indicated in the chart. Now continue working without any additional decreases on the following rounds. Close the heel either with Kitchener stitch, with double-decrease bands, or by pulling the stitches together (see pages 64–65, "Closing the Heel").

PICKING UP STITCHES ON THE SECOND GUSSET SIDE

Pick up the stitches along the loop cast-on, arrange the stitches of Needles 2 and 3 on the double-pointed needles, and knit one round.

Decrease round: knit all the stitches, knit the second and third stitches on Needle 2 together (right slanting), work to 3 stitches from the end of Needle 3, slip the next 2 stitches, knit these stitches together (left slanting), knit 1. Repeat these decreases on every second round until all the gusset stitches have been eliminated.

Continue in rounds for the foot.

Peasant Heel
"Afterthought" heel with a waste yarn . . . medium heel, medium instep

The peasant heel is worked in almost as an afterthought. A great advantage of this heel is that the waste yarn stitches are easy to work and can be removed later. The join to the heel matches the stitches of the heel perfectly and thus is invisible.

Note

One of the advantages of the peasant heel is that it doesn't break up the pattern of self-patterning yarns.

SLIPPING ONTO A HOLDER AND PICKING UP STITCHES WITH A WASTE YARN

Start between the change from Needle 3 to Needle 4. With a waste yarn about 24"/60cm long, knit one row over the stitches on Needles 4 and 1. The working yarn is at the end of Needle 3.

With the working yarn, knit across the row with the waste yarn and continue the foot as if the heel had been worked.

Incorporating the waste yarn

Continuing over the waste

When the sock is complete, remove the waste yarn stitch by stitch, and slip the open stitches evenly onto 4 double-pointed needles. Check to make sure the arrangement of the stitches is correct; there should be the same number of stitches on each needle. The round starts at the center of the lower heel (sole side). This is the start of Needle 1.

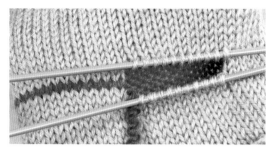

First remove the waste yarn, then pick up the stitches.

NUMBER OF STITCHES FOR "AFTERTHOUGHT" HEEL DECREASES AND CLOSURE WITH FINGERING/4-PLY SOCK YARN

1¾ oz./50g, 230 yards/210m, 30 stitches x 42 rows = 4"/10cm

Children's and women's sizes	5/5½	6/7	8/9	9½/10	11/11½	12/13	1/2	3/4	5/6	7/8	9/9½	10/11	12/13	14/15
Men's sizes										5/6	7/8	9/10	11/12	13/14
Continental sizes	20/21	22/23	24/25	26/27	28/29	30/31	32/33	34/35	36/37	38/39	40/41	42/43	44/45	46/47
Total stitches/ per needle	44/11	44/11	48/12	48/12	52/13	52/13	56/14	56/14	60/15	60/15	64/16	64/16	68/17	72/18
Length of foot from waste yarn to start of toes*	3"	3¼"	3¾"	4¼"	4½"	5"	5"	5½"	5¾"	6"	6¼"	6¾"	6¾"	7"

Repeat the decrease rounds after the 1st decrease round

on every 4th round									once		once		once	once
on every 3rd round	once		once		twice		twice		twice		twice		twice	twice
on every 2nd round	3 times		3 times		3 times		3 times		3 times		3 times		3 times	3 times
on every round			once		once		once		once		twice		once	twice
To close heel, stitches per needle)	6				7								8	

*in relation to the paired toe decreases

NUMBER OF STITCHES FOR "AFTERTHOUGHT" HEEL DECREASES AND CLOSURE WITH DK/6-PLY SOCK YARN

1¾ oz./50g, 137 yards/125m, 22 stitches x 30 rows = 4"/10cm

Children's and women's sizes	5/5½	6/7	8/9	9½/10	11/11 ½	12/13	1/2	3/4	5/6	7/8	9/9½	10/11	12/13	14/15
Men's sizes										5/6	7/8	9/10	11/12	13/14
Continental sizes	20/21	22/23	24/25	26/27	28/29	30/31	32/33	34/35	36/37	38/39	40/41	42/43	44/45	46/47
Total stitches/ per needle	44/11	44/11	48/12	48/12	52/13	52/13	56/14	56/14	60/15	60/15	64/16	64/16	68/17	72/18
Length of foot from waste yarn to start of toes*	4¼"	4¾"	5"	5½"	6"	6½"	6¾"	7¼"	7½"	8"	8½"	9"	9½"	9¾"

Repeat the decrease rounds after the 1st decrease round

on every 4th round					once		once		once		twice		once	twice
on every 3rd round					once		once		once		twice		once	twice
on every 2nd round	3 times		3 times		3 times		3 times		3 times		3 times		3 times	3 times
on every round	once		twice		twice		twice		3 times		3 times		twice	3 times
To close heel, stitches per needle	3						4						5	

*in relation to the paired toe decreases

Tip

The transition to the heel is a lot neater if the horizontal strand on the stitches between the upper foot and the sole—in other words, the stitches between Needles 1 and 2 and Needles 3 and 4—are doubly shortened. To do this, knit together the last stitch on Needles 1 and 3, the first stitch on Needles 2 and 4, together with the twisted horizontal strand.

HEEL DECREASES AND CLOSING THE HEEL

Decrease round: knit across all the stitches, work to 3 stitches from the end of Needles 1 and 3 and knit the next 2 stitches together (right slanting), knit 1. Slip the second and third stitches on Needles 2 and 4 and knit together (left slanting).

Repeat these decreases as indicated in the chart. Now continue without working any additional rounds. Close the heel either with Kitchener stitch, with double-decrease bands, or by pulling the stitches together (see pages 64–65, "Closing the Heel"). The sock is finished!

"Afterthought" Heel with a Waste Yarn
. . . medium heel, medium instep

If you'd rather not work with open stitches on an otherwise complete sock, you can cast on the stitches needed using the loop cast-on method (see page 27). In this case, however, the row of stitches from the loop cast-on method remains slightly visible under the sole of the foot.

If you choose the invisible cast-on method (see page 27), the join remains invisible, but removing the crocheted chain leaves open stitches again. However, if you remove the crocheted chain slowly and carefully, the stitches can be picked up very easily.

The starting point is the end of Needle 3 where the heel begins.

Leave the stitches of Needle 4 on one side.

CASTING ON WITH THE LOOP CAST-ON METHOD

Cast on an equal number of stitches onto 2 double-pointed needles with the working yarn and continue working the sock over 4 needles. When the sock is finished, pick up the stitches of the waste yarn and continue the heel over the cast-on stitches and the stitches that were left on one side.

ALTERNATELY: CASTING ON USING THE INVISIBLE CAST-ON METHOD

Instead of casting on with the loop cast-on method, you can cast on new stitches using the invisible cast-on method instead (see page 27).

When removing the waste yarn, undo only 1 stitch at a time; this stitch can be picked up easily. The join at the heel fits perfectly into the stitch pattern and is completely invisible.

HEEL DECREASES AND HEEL CLOSURE

Work the heel decreases and the closure the same as for the peasant heel. The decreases are indicated in the charts on page 68 for that heel.

Decrease round: knit all the stitches, work to 3 stitches from the end of Needles 1 and 3, knit the 2 stitches together (right slanting), knit 1. Slip the second and third stitches on Needles 2 and 4, knit the stitches together (left slanting). Repeat these decreases as indicated in the chart. Close the heel without working any additional rounds, either with Kitchener stitch, with double-decrease bands, or by pulling the stitches together (see pages 64–65, "Closing the Heel"). The sock is finished!

TOES

Toes should be very durable and also fit very well since the shape of the foot plays a very important role. Toes are somewhat different in length. Depending on the shape of the foot chosen, the toes can be either pointy, rounded, pointy with a blunt end, or anatomically shaped.

Paired-Decrease Toes

Paired-decrease toes are the standard method of finishing toes. They get their characteristic appearance from right-slanting and left-slanting decreases. If the number of rounds between the decrease rounds is reduced toward the toe, they will form a nice rounded toe.

Paired-decrease toe from the front

Paired-decrease toe from the side

continue on page 72

DECREASE ROUNDS FOR PAIRED-DECREASE TOES

Knit all stitches, work to 3 stitches from the end of Needles 1 and 3 and knit the next 2 stitches together (right slanting), knit 1. Knit the second and third stitches on Needles 2 and 4 together (left slanting).

Work these decrease rounds and additional rounds for the respective size for a rounded shape as given in the following charts.

NUMBER OF STITCHES FOR TOES WITH PAIRED-DECREASE TOES WITH FINGERING/4-PLY SOCK YARN
1¾ oz./50g, 230 yards/210m, 30 stitches x 42 rows = 4"/10cm

Children's and women's sizes	5/5½	6/7	8/9	9½/10	11/11½	12/13	1/2	3/4	5/6	7/8	9/9½	10/11	12/13	14/15
Men's sizes										5/6	7/8	9/10	11/12	13/14
Continental sizes	20/21	22/23	24/25	26/27	28/29	30/31	32/33	34/35	36/37	38/39	40/41	42/43	44/45	46/47
Total stitches/per needle	44/11	44/11	48/12	48/12	52/13	52/13	56/14	56/14	60/15	60/15	64/16	64/16	68/17	72/18
Length of foot to toe	4¼"	4¾"	5"	5½"	6"	6½"	6¾"	7¼"	7¾"	8"	8½"	9"	9¼"	9½"
on every 4th round									once		once		once	once
on every 3rd round	once		once		twice		twice		twice		twice		twice	twice
on every 2nd round	3 times		3 times		3 times		3 times		3 times		3 times		4 times	4 times
on every round	4 times		5 times		5 times		6 times		6 times		7 times		7 times	8 times
Stitches per needle (blunt end)			4				5				6			7

71

NUMBER OF STITCHES FOR PAIRED-DECREASE TOES WITH DK/6-PLY SOCK YARN
1¾ oz./50g, 137 yards/125m, 22 stitches x 30 rows = 4"/10cm

Children's and women's sizes	5/5½	6/7	8/9	9½/10	11/11½	12/13	1/2	3/4	5/6	7/8	9/9½	10/11	12/13	14/15
Men's sizes										5/6	7/8	9/10	11/12	13/14
Continental sizes	20/21	22/23	24/25	26/27	28/29	30/31	32/33	34/35	36/37	38/39	40/41	42/43	44/45	46/47
Total stitches/ per needle	44/11	44/11	48/12	48/12	52/13	52/13	56/14	56/14	60/15	60/15	64/16	64/16	68/17	72/18
Length of foot to toe	4¼"	4¾"	5"	5½"	6"	6½"	6¾"	7¼"	7¾"	8"	8½"	9"	9½"	9¾"
on every 4th round														once
on every 3rd round	once		once		once		once		once		twice		twice	once
on every 2nd round	twice		twice		3 times		3 times		4 times		4 times		3 times	3 times
on every round	twice		3 times		3 times		4 times		4 times		4 times		5 times	6 times
Stitches per needle (blunt end)			3				4				5			6

CLOSING TOES BY PULLING STITCHES TOGETHER

After decreasing the number of stitches indicated in the chart, 2 stitches remain on each needle after the last decrease. Cut the working yarn, thread it onto a blunt embroidery needle, and pull the yarn through the 8 band stitches to close (see page 64, "Closing the Heel by Pulling Stitches Together"), and weave in the yarn tail.

CLOSING SHORT PAIRED-DECREASE TOES WITH KITCHENER STITCH

For the short paired-decrease toe, work the decrease bands only until the number of stitches on the needles correspond to the number of stitches indicated in the chart. Then work 1 additional round and join the stitches together with Kitchener stitch.

Additional: knit all the stitches, knit the last 2 stitches on Needles 1 and 3 together (right slanting), slip the first 2 stitches on Needles 2 and 4 and knit the stitches together (left slanting). This additional round prevents "ears" from forming.

Work the stitches on Needle 1 once more to arrive at the side edge. Hold the two rows of stitches to be joined together one behind the other and close using Kitchener stitch (see page 15, "Grafting, or Kitchener Stitch").

Blunt toe shaping (used in star toes or spiral toes) from the front

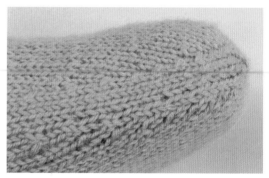

Blunt toe from the side

Anatomically Shaped Toes

Anatomically shaped socks are perfect for people with especially large toes (see the photograph on page 108).

RIGHT SOCK

Work the decrease rounds over the stitches on Needles 1 and 2 as usual as indicated in the chart; work the stitches on Needles 3 and 4 in stockinette stitch without any decreases. On the decrease round before the last additional round start to decrease over the stitches on Needles 3 and 4, and decrease in pattern as you did on Needles 1 and 2. After working all the decrease rounds, join the stitches either with Kitchener stitch or by pulling the stitches together (see page 64, "Closing the Heel by Pulling Stitches Together").

LEFT SOCK

Work the left sock in reverse, working the regular toe decrease rounds over the stitches on Needles 3 and 4, first and then the decreases over the stitches on Needles 1 and 2.

Star Toes

After the paired-decrease toes, the star toes are the most popular toe shaping. Since the decreases are distributed evenly across the toes, star toes are slightly stronger and softer than the band toes. If the decreases are worked as a slip decrease or knitted with a left slant, they form a pattern. If you work them with a right slant, the decreases are hardly visible.

Star toe from the front

Star toe from the side

Finished!

Star toe shaping requires an even number of stitches on each needle. Extra stitches will have been decreased a few rows before the toe shaping is started.

Decrease 2 stitches on each needle on every decrease round. Arrange the stitches on 2 needles (even number of stitches).

DECREASE ROUND

Knit the first 2 stitches of the first half and the first 2 stitches of the second half of each needle together.

The number of rounds worked in stockinette stitch as additional rounds without decreases over the decrease rounds now corresponds to the number of stitches worked in stockinette stitch between the 2 decreases.

Rule of thumb: work as many rounds between the decreases as there are stitches between the decreases. Continue to decrease in pattern until just 8 stitches remain, cut the working yarn, pull the yarn through the remaining 8 stitches to close, weave in the yarn tail.

Example

60 stitches/15 stitches on each needle
Knit the first and second stitches on each needle together,
knit 6 rounds—now start with the toes
knit 2 stitches together, knit 5 stitches,
  work 5 rounds in stockinette stitch
knit 2 stitches together, knit 4 stitches,
  work 4 rounds in stockinette stitch

knit 2 stitches together, knit 3 stitches,
  work 3 rounds in stockinette stitch
knit 2 stitches together, knit 2 stitches,
  work 2 rounds in stockinette stitch
knit 2 stitches together, knit 1 stitch,
  work one round in stockinette stitch
knit 2 stitches together

NUMBER OF STITCHES FOR STAR TOE SHAPING DECREASES WITH FINGERING/4-PLY SOCK YARN
1³/₄ oz./50g, 230 yards/210m, 30 stitches x 42 rows = 4"/10cm

Children's and women's sizes	5/5¹/₂	6/7	8/9	9¹/₂/10	11/11¹/₂	12/13	1/2	3/4	5/6	7/8	9/9¹/₂	10/11	12/13	14/15
Men's sizes										5/6	7/8	9/10	11/12	13/14
Continental sizes	20/21	22/23	24/25	26/27	28/29	30/31	32/33	34/35	36/37	38/39	40/41	42/43	44/45	46/47
Length of foot to toe	4¹/₂"	5"	5"	5¹/₂"	6"	6³/₄"	6³/₄"	7¹/₄"	7³/₄"	8¹/₄"	8"	8¹/₂"	9"	8³/₄"
Total stitches/ per needle	44/11	44/11	48/12	48/12	52/13	52/13	56/14	56/14	60/15	60/15	64/16	64/16	68/17	72/18
	decrease needed				decrease needed				decrease needed				decrease needed	
No. of stitches/ per toes	40/10	40/10	48/12	48712	48/12	48/12	56/14	56/14	56/14	57/14	64/16	64/16	64/16	72/18
No. of stitches between decreases of 1st decrease round	3		4				5				6			7

NUMBER OF STITCHES FOR STAR TOE SHAPING DECREASES WITH DK/6-PLY SOCK YARN
1³/₄ oz./50g, 137 yards/125m, 22 stitches x 30 rows = 4"/10cm

Children's and women's sizes	5/5¹/₂	6/7	8/9	9¹/₂/10	11/11¹/₂	12/13	1/2	3/4	5/6	7/8	9/9¹/₂	10/11	12/13	14/15
Men's sizes										5/6	7/8	9/10	11/12	13/14
Continental sizes	20/21	22/23	24/25	26/27	28/29	30/31	32/33	34/35	36/37	38/39	40/41	42/43	44/45	46/47
Length of foot to toe	4¹/₄"	4³/₄"	5"	5¹/₂"	6"	6¹/₂"	6³/₄"	7¹/₄"	7³/₄"	8"	8¹/₂"	9"	9¹/₂"	9³/₄"
Total stitches/ per needle	32/8	32/8	36/9	36/9	40/10	40/10	44/11	44/11	48/12	48/12	52/13	52/13	52/13	56/14
			decrease needed				decrease needed				decrease needed			
No. of stitches/ per toes	32/8	32/8	32/8	40/10	40/10	40/10	40/10	40/10	48/12	48/12	48/12	48/12	48/12	56/14
No. of stitches between decreases of 1st decrease round	2		3					4						5

Spiral Toes

This toe shaping is especially good for pointy feet and is also very durable. The spiral toe is very easy to work and doesn't involve too much counting. The decreases look very pretty if you decide to show them. Work the decreases in rounds. There is no noticeable seam.

Spiral toe from the front

Spiral toe from the side

DECREASE ROUND

Slip the first stitch of each needle, knit the second stitch, pass the slipped stitch over the knitted stitch. Work one round in stockinette stitch.

Slip the second stitch of each needle, knit the third stitch, pass the slipped stitch over the knitted stitch. Work one round in stockinette stitch.

Slip the third stitch of each needle, knit the fourth stitch, pass the slipped stitch over the knitted stitch. Work one round in stockinette stitch.

Repeat in pattern until just 8 stitches remain on the needles. Pull the stitches together with the working yarn, and weave in the yarn tail.

NUMBER OF STITCHES FOR SPIRAL TOE SHAPING DECREASES WITH FINGERING/4-PLY SOCK YARN
1³/₄ oz./50g, 230 yards/210m, 30 stitches x 42 rows = 4"/10cm

Children's and women's sizes	5/5½	6/7	8/9	9½/10	11/11½	12/13	1/2	3/4	5/6	7/8	9/9½	10/11	12/13	14/15
Men's sizes										5/6	7/8	9/10	11/12	13/14
Continental sizes	20/21	22/23	24/25	26/27	28/29	30/31	32/33	34/35	36/37	38/39	40/41	42/43	44/45	46/47
Total stitches/ per needle	44/11	44/11	48/12	48/12	52/13	52/13	56/14	56/14	60/15	60/15	64/16	64/16	68/17	72/18
Length of foot to toe	3³/₄"	4¼"	4³/₄"	5"	5½"	6"	6¼"	6³/₄"	7¼"	7³/₄"	8"	8½"	8³/₄"	9¼"

NUMBER OF STITCHES FOR SPIRAL TOE SHAPING DECREASES WITH DK/6-PLY SOCK YARN
1³/₄ oz./50g, 137 yards/125m, 22 stitches x 30 rows = 4"/10cm

Children's and women's sizes	5/5½	6/7	8/9	9½/10	11/11 ½	12/13	1/2	3/4	5/6	7/8	9/9½	10/11	12/13	14/15
Men's sizes										5/6	7/8	9/10	11/12	13/14
Continental sizes	20/21	22/23	24/25	26/27	28/29	30/31	32/33	34/35	36/37	38/39	40/41	42/43	44/45	46/47
Total stitches/ per needle	32/8	32/8	36/9	36/9	40/10	40/10	44/11	44/11	48/12	48/12	52/13	52/13	52/13	56/14
Length of foot to toe	4"	4½"	5"	5¼"	5³/₄"	6¼"	6¼"	6³/₄"	7¼"	7³/₄"	8"	8½"	9"	8³/₄"

Flower Toes

This toe is round and is suitable for all feet. Originally the decreases for this toe were worked on every second round, which led to the flower toe being considerably shorter than other toes. Today, however, we work 3 rows between each decrease round so that the toe shaping has a better fit. The attractive pattern is also more visible this way. Like the decreases for the spiral toes and the propeller toes, the decreases for the flower toes are distributed over the entire foot.

Flower toe from the front

Flower toe from the side

DECREASE ROUND

Work the following decreases on each of the 4 double-pointed needles:

Round 1: Purl the first 2 stitches together, knit the rest of the stitches.

Work 3 rounds.

On the next decrease round also purl the last 2 stitches together.

Round 5: Knit all the stitches, purl the second and third stitches together, continue knitting to the last 2 stitches, purl the last 2 stitches together.

Work 3 rounds.

Round 9: Knit all the stitches, purl the third and fourth stitches together, continue knitting until the last 2 stitches, purl the last 2 stitches together.

Work 3 rounds.

Round 13: Knit all the stitches, purl the fourth and fifth stitches together, continue knitting until the last 2 stitches, purl the last 2 stitches together.

Work 2 rounds.

Continue in pattern until the 2 purl decreases at the end of the needle are next to one another.

Knit all the stitches, slip the last unworked stitch. Knit the first stitch on the next needle, pass the slipped stitch over.

Repeat these decreases on every round until just 8 stitches remain. Pull these stitches together with the working yarn to close, and weave in the yarn end.

NUMBER OF STITCHES FOR FLOWER TOE SHAPING DECREASES WITH FINGERING/4-PLY SOCK YARN
1¾ oz./50g, 230 yards/210m, 30 stitches x 42 rows = 4"/10cm

Children's and women's sizes	5/5½	6/7	8/9	9½/10	11/11½	12/13	1/2	3/4	5/6	7/8	9/9½	10/11	12/13	14/15
Men's sizes										5/6	7/8	9/10	11/12	13/14
Continental sizes	20/21	22/23	24/25	26/27	28/29	30/31	32/33	34/35	36/37	38/39	40/41	42/43	44/45	46/47
Total stitches/per needle	44/11	44/11	48/12	48/12	52/13	52/13	56/14	56/14	60/15	60/15	64/16	64/16	68/17	72/18
Length of foot to toe	4"	4½"	5¼"	5½"	6"	6½"	6¾"	7½"	7¾"	8"	8¾"	9¼"	9½"	10"

NUMBER OF STITCHES FOR FLOWER TOE SHAPING DECREASES WITH DK/6-PLY SOCK YARN
1¾ oz./50g, 137 yards/125m, 22 stitches x 30 rows = 4"/10cm

Children's and women's sizes	5/5½	6/7	8/9	9½/10	11/11½	12/13	1/2	3/4	5/6	7/8	9/9½	10/11	12/13	14/15
Men's sizes										5/6	7/8	9/10	11/12	13/14
Continental sizes	20/21	22/23	24/25	26/27	28/29	30/31	32/33	34/35	36/37	38/39	40/41	42/43	44/45	46/47
Total stitches/per needle	32/8	32/8	36/9	36/9	40/10	40/10	44/11	44/11	48/12	48/12	52/13	52/13	52/13	56/14
Length of foot to toe	4¼"	5"	5¼"	5½"	6"	6¾"	6¾"	7¼"	7¾"	8¼"	8½"	9"	9½"	10"

Diagonal Seam Heel for Toes

This toe shaping is worked the same as for a heel with a diagonal seam. Short-row heels with reinforced double stitches (see page 56), wrap stitch heels (see page 58) and mock short-row heels (see page 63) are especially suitable. The diagonal seam heel toe is a blunt toe that easily adapts to the shape of the toes.

Short-row heel with reinforced double stitches from the front

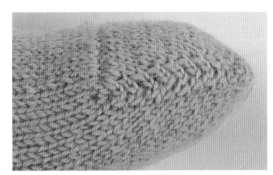

Short-row heel with reinforced double stitches from the side

Short-row heel with reinforced double stitches as a heel

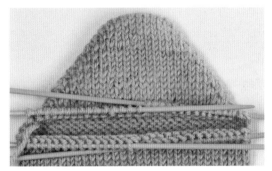

Short-row heel with reinforced double stitches as a toe

Unlike the other toes, the diagonal seam heel is worked in short rows for the toe. Leave the stitches on Needles 4 and 1 on one side, and work the diagonal seam heel over the stitches on Needles 2 and 3 for the toes. When the toe/heel is complete, the stitches on Needles 2 and 3 meet the stitches on Needles 4 and 1 and can be joined either with Kitchener stitch or by being pulled together (see pages 64–65, "Closing the Heel").

NUMBER OF STITCHES FOR DIAGONAL SEAM HEEL FOR TOE SHAPING WITH FINGERING/4-PLY SOCK YARN
1³/₄ oz./50g, 230 yards/210m, 30 stitches x 42 rows = 4"/10cm

Children's and women's sizes	5/5½	6/7	8/9	9½/10	11/11½	12/13	1/2	3/4	5/6	7/8	9/9½	10/11	12/13	14/15
Men's sizes										5/6	7/8	9/10	11/12	13/14
Continental sizes	20/21	22/23	24/25	26/27	28/29	30/31	32/33	34/35	36/37	38/39	40/41	42/43	44/45	46/47
No. of stitches per needle	7/8/7	7/8/7	8/8/8	8/8/8	9/8/9	9/8/9	10/8/10	10/8/10	11/8/11	11/8/11	11/10/11	11/10/11	12/10/12	13/10/13
Length of foot to toe	4¹/₄"	4³/₄"	5¹/₄"	5¹/₂"	6"	6¹/₂"	6³/₄"	7¹/₄"	7³/₄"	8"	8³/₄"	9¹/₄"	9¹/₂"	10"

NUMBER OF STITCHES FOR DIAGONAL SEAM HEEL FOR TOE SHAPING WITH DK/6-PLY SOCK YARN
1³/₄ oz./50g, 137 yards/125m, 22 stitches x 30 rows = 4"/10cm

Children's and women's sizes	5/5½	6/7	8/9	9½/10	11/11½	12/13	1/2	3/4	5/6	7/8	9/9½	10/11	12/13	14/15
Men's sizes										5/6	7/8	9/10	11/12	13/14
Continental sizes	20/21	22/23	24/25	26/27	28/29	30/31	32/33	34/35	36/37	38/39	40/41	42/43	44/45	46/47
No. of stitches per needle	5/6/5	5/6/5	6/6/6	6/6/6	6/8/6	6/8/6	7/8/7	7/8/7	8/8/8	8/8/8	9/9/9	9/9/9	9/9/9	9/10/9
Length of foot to toe	4¹/₄"	4³/₄"	5¹/₄"	5¹/₂	6"	6³/₄"	7"	7¹/₂"	8"	8¹/₂"	8¹/₂"	9"	9¹/₂"	10"

CLOSING THE TOES WITH KITCHENER STITCH

Slip the stitches of the 2 heel needles (Needles 4 and 1) onto one needle and the stitches of the 2 sole needles (Needles 2 and 3) onto a spare needle. Hold the two needles one behind the other, and join the stitches using Kitchener stitch (see page 15, "Grafting, or Kitchener Stitch").

CLOSING THE TOES BY KNITTING STITCHES TOGETHER

Tip

The seam should always be under the foot so that it doesn't press against the toes.

Carefully turn the socks inside out and slip all the stitches onto one needle: starting at the side opposite to the working yarn, slip the stitches to be joined alternately onto one needle. Now knit 2 stitches together across the row.

Sock turned inside out to knit stitches together

Propeller Toes

This toe shaping is for very pointy feet. This toe is very easy to work even without doing much counting. The decreases are done just once on each needle.

Propeller toe from the front

Propeller toe from the side

DECREASE ROUND

Knit the first 2 stitches on each needle together. Repeat these decreases on every second round. When just ¹⁄₃ of the original number of stitches remains, omit the additional rounds. Cut the working yarn, pull the yarn through the last 8 stitches to close, and weave in the yarn tail.

Example

60 stitches/15 stitches on each needle
   10 decrease rounds with additional rounds, 3 decrease rounds without additional rounds, pull 2 stitches together on each needle at the end.

NUMBER OF STITCHES FOR PROPELLER TOE SHAPING WITH FINGERING/4-PLY SOCK YARN
1¾ oz./50g, 230 yards/210m, 30 stitches x 42 rows = 4"/10cm

Children's and women's sizes	5/5½	6/7	8/9	9½/10	11½	12/13	1/2	3/4	5/6	7/8	9/9½	10/11	12/13	14/15
Men's sizes										5/6	7/8	9/10	11/12	13/14
Continental sizes	20/21	22/23	24/25	26/27	28/29	30/31	32/33	34/35	36/37	38/39	40/41	42/43	44/45	46/47
Total stitches/ per needle	44/11	44/11	48/12	48/12	52/13	52/13	56/14	56/14	60/15	60/15	64/16	64/16	68/17	72/18
Length of foot to toe	3¾"	4¼"	4¾"	5"	5½"	6"	6½"	7"	7½"	8"	8¼"	8¾"	9"	9½"

NUMBER OF STITCHES FOR PROPELLER TOE SHAPING WITH DK/6-PLY SOCK YARN
1¾ oz./50g, 137 yards/125m, 22 stitches x 30 rows = 4"/10cm

Children's and women's sizes	5/5½	6/7	8/9	9½/10	11½	12/13	1/2	3/4	5/6	7/8	9/9½	10/11	12/13	14/15
Men's sizes										5/6	7/8	9/10	11/12	13/14
Continental sizes	20/21	22/23	24/25	26/27	28/29	30/31	32/33	34/35	36/37	38/39	40/41	42/43	44/45	46/47
Total stitches/ per needle	32/8	32/8	36/9	36/9	40/10	40/10	44/11	44/11	48/12	48/12	52/13	52/13	52/13	56/14
Length of foot to toe	4"	4½"	5"	5¼"	5¾"	6¼"	6½"	7"	7½"	7¾"	8¼"	8¾"	9"	9½"

TIPS FOR THE LENGTH OF THE FOOT TO THE START OF THE TOE SHAPING

For an overview of all the toe measurements, see the charts at the end of the book, pages 121–122 and 124–125.

For a wider foot it is often recommended that you use the measurements for the next size up, thereby starting with 1 stitch more on each needle. But that changes not just the width of the foot and the leg, but also the size of the heel and the toes, so that the completed socks can have creases later when they are in the shoes.

Preferable options:
For a wider foot it is usually enough to add 3 to 4 rounds to the length of the foot before starting the toe shaping, thereby utilizing the elasticity of the fabric.

For a very wide foot, it might be preferable to work the foot, the toe, and the heel over more stitches. However, in this case you should keep to the original size for the length of the foot to the start of the toes and not to the length corresponding to the number of stitches.

OTHER SOCK KNITTING TECHNIQUES

Even when knitting socks, it's still worthwhile to look farther than the end of one's nose (or toes)—there is an amazing amount to be discovered. From the Balkan states to Turkey and Iran, and right up to Afghanistan, from Egypt to Ukraine, socks are traditionally knitted from the toe up and worked up to the leg. Again and again we find instructions for working socks on just two needles. A good alternative to using double-pointed needles is to use circular needles instead.

TOE-UP SOCKS— STARTING AT THE TOES

These socks are worked up from the toes on double-pointed needles. In Turkey it is usual to work socks up from the toes rather than to start them at the cuff. When finished, the socks may look like any other pair, but starting at the toes does have certain advantages.

If you work your socks from the top down, as is usual in the West, any pattern would obviously be on its head. This doesn't really show in the case of symmetrical patterns, and even color patterns can be worked from the top down. But some textured patterns just won't allow themselves to be turned the other way around on the leg. This is especially true for leaf patterns. Some knitters prefer this method of working socks, especially when they want to use up some special yarns they have left over and don't want to run out halfway down the foot. A shorter leg is easier to accommodate than an unfinished foot.

Working toe-up socks requires the following:

- casting on toes
- suitable heels
- very elastic means of binding off

The number of stitches for the various sizes and yarns remains the same for almost all methods of working. However, for toe-up socks, the decreases for the toes have to be worked as increases.

Since the specific method used for decreasing for the toes is simply worked in the opposite direction (= from the toes up to the foot), the arrangement of the decreases in the round and the number of rows in between the decreases also remains the same.

Toe-Up Toes

Casting on and working only a few stitches across 4 double-pointed needles might initially need a little getting used to, but this method is familiar in the West.

FIGURE EIGHT CAST-ON

Wind the yarn around 2 double-pointed needles in figure eights until there are 4 stitches on each needle. These 8 loops are the start of the sock and do not form a hole at the front of the toes.

Knit the first 4 loops with a third needle, twist the needles 180 degrees, and knit the 4 loops with the second needle. Arrange the stitches evenly across 4 double-pointed needles and work a sock toe in reverse.

Work the decreases of a normal toe in reverse, working increases for decreases.

The foundation stitches will become a little wider when they are knit, so now tighten them one by one to carefully bring them back to the original stitch size with the initial yarn tail.

Example Star Toes

There are 2 stitches on each needle.
make 1 into the horizontal strand, knit 1,
  work one round without increases.
make 1 into the horizontal strand, knit 2,
  work 2 rounds without increases.
make 1 into the horizontal strand, knit 3,
  work 3 rounds without increases.
make 1 into the horizontal strand, knit 4,
  work 4 rounds without increases.
make 1 into the horizontal strand, knit 5,
  work 5 rounds without increases.
  etc.

Tip

Keep track of your rounds by marking Needle 1. Attach a stitch marker behind the first stitch on Needle 1.

Note

For a wedge toe (a non-pointed toe with diagonal toe-shaping), cast on more stitches on each needle. Use these to work the double-decrease band in reverse.

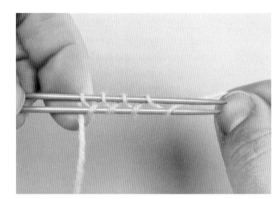

Figure eight cast-on

The first round after the figure eight cast-on

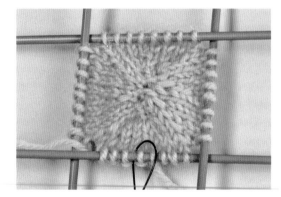

A few rounds in reverse star toe pattern with figure eight cast-on

CASTING ON WITH A LOOP

Make a loop around the index finger of your left hand, bring the yarn over the outstretched thumb, and hold the yarn tail and the working yarn with your middle finger, ring finger, and pinky finger.

Insert the needle into the double loop from right to left and bring the working yarn through, then bring the yarn over the double loop. Continue until there are 6 stitches on the needle.

Pick up another 6 stitches with a second needle. Hold the stitches close together and parallel to each other and separate the yarns if they have become tangled. Do not knot the yarn tail.

Work the 12 stitches and arrange them evenly across 4 needles, mark Needle 1 with a stitch marker (= insert the marker after the first stitch).

Knit 1, make 1 knitwise through the back of the horizontal strand, knit 2. Check to make sure that the loop can still be pulled tight when the yarn tail is pulled through, but do not close the loop completely yet. If it is not possible to close the loop, cast on the stitches again rather than have a hole in the toes later.

The toe-up toe method is hard to distinguish from the Western method of working toes.

Note

Since there is little room to move, especially when working the first few rounds of toe-up socks, it might be easier to work the increases into the stitch.

To do this, knit or purl the last stitch before an increase in pattern, insert the left-hand needle into the last stitch of the previous row or round (not into the loop of the right-hand needle) from back to front, and knit or purl.

Making a loop

Alternate 1 stitch, 1 yarn-over.

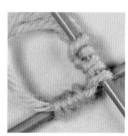
6 stitches on each needle

First round after casting on

Continue in rounds, working a reverse star toe (= working increases for decreases, and working from the bottom up).

The loop will loosen occasionally while you are knitting.

When the work is the correct size, weave in the loop on the inside.

A few rounds in reverse star toe shaping with loop

Reverse star toe

MOCK HEEL

A neat and easy way to work a sock from the toes up is to work a heel with a diagonal seam for the toe. The wrap stitch heel, the heel with reinforced double stitches, and the mock short-row heel are all very well suited since the diagonal seams of these heels are especially strong, hole-free and durable (see page 52, "Heels with Diagonal Seams"). The toe starts under the foot and is formed around the toes. Initially it is worked over just half the number of stitches.

Using the invisible cast-on (see page 27), first cast on half the number of stitches needed. We always recommend working the crocheted chain a few stitches longer, because this should prevent the stitches from unraveling.

Make sure you pick up the stitches through the back of the horizontal strands of the crocheted chain stitches; otherwise the chain stitches will be very difficult to undo.

Finally, work a heel with diagonal seams. The photograph shows the finished toe (mock heel) from the side, since it also looks like a heel. If you put the foundation edge on top of the working row, you will recognize the toe shaping. The crocheted chain along the foundation edge still holds the stitches in place.

Remove the crocheted chain 1 stitch at a time and pick up the free stitches. Since the stitches are staggered by half a stitch when the invisible cast-on method is used, you will lose half a stitch at each end. To compensate for this, pick up 1 more stitch through the back of a horizontal strand between 2 stitches.

Arrange the stitches evenly across 4 double-pointed needles and continue with the sock toward the heel.

Diagonal seam heel with invisible cast-on as the toe for a toe-up sock

Remove the crocheted chain and pick up the stitches.

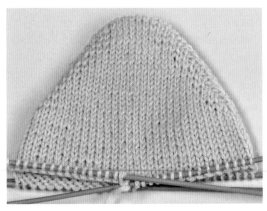

Mock heel as toes, with stitches arranged evenly across 4 needles

DIAGONAL TOE SHAPING USING THE INVISIBLE CAST-ON METHOD

A short toe band starts at the toes and continues in rounds around the toes and foot.

Work an invisible cast-on with as many stitches as are indicated in the chart and work 4 rows in stockinette stitch. Arrange the stitches evenly across 2 needles, remove the waste yarn, and arrange these stitches evenly across 2 more needles, then pick up 1 stitch through the back of a horizontal strand along one side so that each of the 4 needles has the same number of stitches. Continue in rounds.

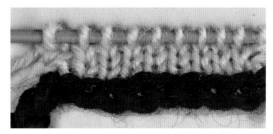

Cast-on with 4 rows

Increase Round

Make 1 knitwise through the back of the horizontal strand in front of the last stitch on Needles 1 and 3 and after the first stitch on Needles 2 and 4. Repeat this increase on every second round, or, for a rounded toe, in reverse to the double-decrease toes until you have the number of stitches needed for the foot.

After working a few increase rounds

Toe bands from the top

Toe bands from the side

NUMBER OF STITCHES FOR CASTING ON FOR DIAGONAL TOES WITH FINGERING/4-PLY SOCK YARN
1³/₄ oz./50g, 230 yards/210m, 30 stitches x 42 rows = 4"/10cm

Children's and women's sizes	5/5½	6/7	8/9	9½/10	11/11½	12/13	1/2	3/4	5/6	7/8	9/9½	10/11	12/13	14/15
Men's sizes										5/6	7/8	9/10	11/12	13/14
Continental sizes	20/21	22/23	24/25	26/27	28/29	30/31	32/33	34/35	36/37	38/39	40/41	42/43	44/45	46/47
Total stitches/ per needle	44/11	44/11	48/12	48/12	52/13	52/13	56/14	56/14	60/15	60/15	64/16	64/16	68/17	72/18
Total stitches cast on	6						8				10			

NUMBER OF STITCHES FOR CASTING ON FOR DIAGONAL TOES WITH DK/6-PLY SOCK YARN
1³/₄ oz./50g, 137 yards/125m, 22 stitches x 30 rows = 4"/10cm

Children's and women's sizes	5/5½	6/7	8/9	9½/10	11/11½	12/13	1/2	3/4	5/6	7/8	9/9½	10/11	12/13	14/15
Men's sizes										5/6	7/8	9/10	11/12	13/14
Continental sizes	20/21	22/23	24/25	26/27	28/29	30/31	32/33	34/35	36/37	38/39	40/41	42/43	44/45	46/47
Total stitches/ per needle	32/8	32/8	36/9	36/9	40/10	40/10	44/11	44/11	48/12	48/12	52/13	52/13	52/13	56/14
Total stitches cast on	4						6				8			

HORTIZONTAL TOE BANDS USING THE INVISIBLE CAST-ON METHOD

The horizontal toe bands start as a rectangle worked on 2 needles.

Cast on 6 stitches using the invisible cast-on method and work 20 rows in garter stitch with double-beaded selvages (see page 41, "Double-Beaded Selvage"). Pick up 10 stitches along the double-beaded stitches along each side, remove the crocheted chain, and pick up the free stitches one at a time. Arrange the stitches on double-pointed needles so that there are 3 bands at the end of Needles 1 and 3 and at the beginning of Needles 2 and 4.

Increase Round

With Needles 1 and 3 pick up 1 stitch each through the back of the horizontal strand in front of the garter band stitches, with Needles 2 and 4 pick up 1 stitch each through the back of the horizontal strand after the garter band stitches.

Continue in garter stitch over the band stitches.

Work the increase round either on every second round or in reverse to the respective decreases for this method.

Cast-on stitches arranged on 2 needles

Horizontal toe bands seen from the side

Horizontal toe bands seen from the top

ANY TOE SHAPING USING THE INVISIBLE CAST-ON METHOD

If you work an invisible cast-on for the entire number of stitches needed for a foot, you can work any toe shaping according to the Western method and add the foot, working toward the heel, later. This method is easy for beginning sock knitters too.

For the invisible cast-on, crochet a chain, working 10 chain stitches more than the required number of stitches for the entire foot. Pick up the number of stitches needed one at a time through the back of the horizontal strands, arrange all stitches evenly across 4 double-pointed needles, and join to form a round.

Complete cast-on across 4 needles

Work a toe shaping of your choice and weave in the yarn tail.

Remove the crochet chain and pick up the free stitches one at a time. Arrange the free stitches evenly across the double-pointed needles, and work toward the heel for the foot.

Half-completed toe shaping using invisible cast-on method

Remove the crocheted chain and pick up the stitches.

Heels for Toe-Up Socks

All short-row heels can be worked in the opposite direction without any change in the instructions, even the hybrid heel, the plain heel, and all "afterthought" heels.

LENGTH OF FOOT FROM TOE TO HEEL WITH FINGERING/4-PLY AND DK/6-PLY SOCK YARN

Children's and women's sizes	5/5½	6/7	8/9	9½/10	11/11½	12/13	1/2	3/4	5/6	7/8	9/9½	10/11	12/13	14/15
Men's sizes										5/6	7/8	9/10	11/12	13/14
Continental sizes	20/21	22/23	24/25	26/27	28/29	30/31	32/33	34/35	36/37	38/39	40/41	42/43	44/45	46/47
Heel to toe	4½"	4¾"	4¾"	5¼"	5½"	6"	6½"	6¾"	7"	7¾"	8½"	8¾"	9"	9¾"

When increasing and decreasing for the gusset, including the hybrid heel, any additional length needed for the gusset must be taken into consideration.

These heels cover practically all fitting combinations. Only the heels with heel flaps are problematical, because the heel flaps cannot be reversed. The best fit for a wide heel and medium to high instep for toe-up socks is the heart-shaped heel.

FINDING THE RIGHT TOE-UP HEEL

HEEL	INSTEP	HEEL SHAPE
narrow	low	short-row heel, short-row heel with reinforced double stitches, wrap stitch heel, mock short-row heel
	medium	increase and decrease gusset
	high	hybrid heel
medium	low	short-row heel with round shaping
	medium	standard heel, "afterthought" heel
	high	standard heel
wide	low	short-row heel with round shaping
	medium	heart-shaped toe-up heel
	high	heart-shaped toe-up heel

HEART-SHAPED TOE-UP HEEL

Once the foot has been worked to the required length (see the chart), work the heart-shaped heel.

NUMBER OF STITCHES FOR HEART-SHAPED HEEL FOR TOE-UP SOCKS WITH FINGERING/4-PLY SOCK YARN

1¾ oz./50g, 230 yards/210m, 30 stitches x 42 rows = 4"/10cm

Children's and women's sizes	5/5½	6/7	8/9	9½/10	11/11½	12/13	1/2	3/4	5/6	7/8	9/9½	10/11	12/13	14/15
Men's sizes										5/6	7/8	9/10	11/12	13/14
Continental sizes	20/21	22/23	24/25	26/27	28/29	30/31	32/33	34/35	36/37	38/39	40/41	42/43	44/45	46/47
Total stitches/ per needle	44/11	44/11	48/12	48/12	52/13	52/13	56/14	56/14	60/15	60/15	64/16	64/16	68/17	72/18
Total stitches per heel	22		24		26		28		30		32		34	36
Foot to toe	2¾"	3¼"	3¼"	3½"	4¼"	4¾"	5"	5½"	5½"	6"	6½"	6¾"	7¼"	7¼"
Total stitches per gusset	6		8						10					12
Total stitches before heart	34		40		42		44		50		52		54	70
Total stitches per side panel	11		12		13		14		15		16		17	18

NUMBER OF STITCHES FOR HEART-SHAPED HEEL FOR TOE-UP SOCKS WITH DK/6-PLY SOCK YARN

1¾ oz./50g, 137 yards/125m, 22 stitches x 30 rows = 4"/10cm

Children's and women's sizes	5/5½	6/7	8/9	9½/10	11/11½	12/13	1/2	3/4	5/6	7/8	9/9½	10/11	12/13	14/15
Men's sizes										5/6	7/8	9/10	11/12	13/14
Continental sizes	20/21	22/23	24/25	26/27	28/29	30/31	32/33	34/35	36/37	38/39	40/41	42/43	44/45	46/47
Total stitches/ per needle	32/8	32/8	36/9	36/9	40/10	40/10	44/11	44/11	48/12	48/12	52/13	52/13	52/13	56/14
Total stitches per heel	16		18		20		22		24		26		28	
Foot to toe	2¾"	3¼"	3¼"	3½"	4¼"	4¾"	5"	5½"	5½"	6"	6½"	6¾"	7¼"	7¼"
Total stitches per gusset	4		6						8					
Total stitches before heart	24		30		32		34		40		42		42	44
Total stitches per side panel	8		9		10		11		12		13		13	14

Gusset Increases

Work the gusset increases in rounds.

Increase Round

Knit all the stitches on Needle 1, make 1 through the back of the horizontal strand before the last stitch on Needle 1, work the stitches on Needles 2 and 3 in pattern, knit all the stitches on Needle 4, make 1 through the back of the horizontal strand. Repeat these increases on every second round until you reach the number of stitches on either side as given in the chart.

Continue with the leg over the usual number of stitches.

Reversed Heart

Slip the stitches on Needles 2 and 3 onto one needle. For the reverse heart, work the increases in short rows over the center stitches only. Arrange the heel stitches over the center panel and the two side panels. On either side of the heel stitches (= the stitches on Needles 4 and 1) pick up the side panel stitches with another double-pointed needle and leave on one side (see the charts on page 88, "Number of Stitches for Heart-shaped Heel for Toe-Up Socks").

Start at the center of the heel on a right-side row between Needles 4 and 1. The stitches from Needles 2 and 3 are on one side, the side panels stitches are both on one needle, the center of the heel has already been half worked.

Row 1 (1/2 right-side row): Knit all the stitches until just the 2 center stitches are left unworked. Pick up 1 stitch through the back of the horizontal strand, knit 1, work 1 double stitch.

Row 2 (wrong-side row): Bring the yarn between the needles to the front, purl all the stitches until just the 2 center stitches are left unworked. Pick up 1 stitch through the back of the horizontal strand, purl 1, work 1 double stitch.

Row 3 (right-side row): Knit all the stitches to 2 stitches before the lower increased stitch (there are still 5 stitches at the left edge of the center needle), pick up 1 stitch through the back of the horizontal strand, knit 1, work 1 double stitch.

Row 4 (wrong-side row): Bring the yarn between the needles to the front, purl all the stitches to 2 stitches before the lower increased stitch, pick up 1 stitch through the back of the horizontal strand, purl 1, work 1 double stitch.

Repeat rows 2 and 3 until only 4 stitches remain at the center between the two increases. End with half of a wrong-side row.

Heel Flap

Now work the heel flap over the original center heel stitches.

The working yarn is at the center of the heel. At this point leave half the number of heel stitches on the working needle. Slip the remaining stitches onto another needle for the side pane, and leave the needle on one side. Do the same at the right edge of the heel and make sure that only the heel stitches remain at the center. Half the heel flap has now been worked.

Begin at the center of the heel on a right-side row.

Row 1 (1/2 right-side row): Knit all the stitches, slip the last stitch of the heel flap and the first stitch of the side panel, knit the stitches together (left slanting), turn.

Row 2 (wrong-side row): Slip the first stitch, purl all the stitches, purl the last stitch of the heel flap and the first stitch of the side panel together, turn.

Row 3 (right-side row): Slip the first stitch, knit all the stitches, slip the last stitch of the heel flap and the first stitch of the side panel, knit the stitches together (left slanting), turn.

Row 4 (wrong-side row): Slip the first stitch, purl all the stitches, purl the last stitch of the heel flap and the first stitch of the side panel together, turn.

Repeat rows 3 and 4 until just the original number of heel stitches remain on Needles 1 and 4.

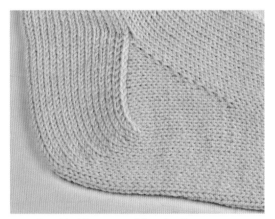

Heart-shaped heel for toe-up sock from the side

Tip

It is possible to reinforce the heel flap of the heart-shaped heel for toe-up socks with a slipped stitch pattern. In this case work a reinforced rib pattern or a reinforced netting pattern between the center heel panel stitches (= the stitches between the stitch markers) (see page 42, "Reinforcing the Heel").

Tip

If you have large calves, work a small roll edge after the cuff. This will be a lot looser when bound off than the traditional ribbing. If you want the sock to be nice and loose, work four more stitches through the back of the horizontal strands on the first row of the roll edge.

Finishes for Toe-Up Socks

Obviously, toe-up sock cuffs need the same elasticity and stretch as any other sock cuff. They should be elastic and keep the sock leg in place, but they should not cut in.

RIGHT SIDE AND WRONG SIDE OF BOUND-OFF EDGE

Just as there is a right side and a wrong side when you are picking up stitches, there is also a right side and a wrong side when you are binding off stitches. If you are binding off in the direction you are working, there will be horizontal strands on the right side of work and small ridges on the wrong side. Also, the right side of the edge will tilt slightly forward or sag, which makes the cuff look slightly worn.

BINDING OFF ON THE WRONG SIDE

If you bind off in the opposite direction, the bound-off edge looks slightly rounded and adheres to the leg nicely. Once the cuff has the desired height, turn the work and bind off all the stitches on Needle 4 and all other needles in the opposite direction from the direction in which you had been working.

STANDARD BIND-OFF

The standard method of binding off is very simple but has to be worked very carefully and loosely to make sure the edge remains elastic.

Pattern sequence

Knit 2
with the left-hand needle slip the first stitch over the second stitch and slip the second stitch off the needle, knit 1

Slip the first stitch over the second stitch.

Knit 1 more stitch.

TWISTED KNIT BIND-OFF

The twisted stitches strengthen the bound-off edge.

Pattern sequence

Knit 2
with the left-hand needle slip the first stitch over the second stitch but leave the second stitch on the left-hand needle, with the right-hand needle knit the second stitch on the left-hand needle through the back of the loop and slip both stitches off the left-hand needle (there is only 1 stitch on the right-hand needle), knit 1

The differences between the right side and the wrong side are easy to see.

Slip the first stitch over the second stitch.

Knit the next stitch through the back of the loop.

Front and back along 1 x 1 rib

DOUBLE KNIT TWISTED BIND-OFF

Binding off 2 stitches through the back of the loops results in a very stretchy edge that is reinforced by the double knit.

Pattern sequence

Knit 2
slip both stitches back onto the left-hand needle and knit the stitches together through back of the loops, knit 1

Knit 1

Knit both stitches together through the back of the loops.

Italian Bind-off

An Italian bind-off forms a round and very elastic finish. There is very little visible difference between the right-side and wrong-side rows, and the finishing edge is not wavy. This finish is not knitted, but rather is sewn with a blunt embroidery needle. As with the Italian method of casting on, 6 transition rounds make this edge very stretchy too.

PREPARING A 2 X 2 RIB

Since this bind-off really only works after the transition rounds of a 1 x 1 rib, a 2 x 2 rib will have to be adjusted so that it can be continued as a 1 x 1 rib.
Work the first 2 stitches of the right-hand needle with Needle 4 and start with 2 purl stitches.

Pattern sequence

purl 1, knit the second following stitch at front of the work (do not slip it), then purl the purl stitch in between, slip the stitches off the needle, knit 1
Continue with the transition rounds of a 1 x 1 rib.

Purl 1, knit the second stitch.

Purl the center stitch.

Twisted stitches

ITALIAN BIND-OFF FOR A 1 X 1 RIB

Additional rounds

Rounds 1, 3, and 5: Knit all the knit stitches, slip the purl stitches with the yarn at the front of the work.
Rounds 2, 4, and 6: Purl all the purl stitches, slip all the knit stitches with the yarn at the back of the work.
   Then bind off the stitches individually.

Step 1

Insert the needle into the purl stitch from left to right and pull the yarn through. Leave the stitch on the needle.

Insert the needle into the purl stitch from left to right.

Step 2

Insert the needle from right to left into the preceding knit stitch, skip the purl stitch that was just worked, insert the needle into the following knit stitch from right to left. Pull the yarn through, leave the stitches on the left-hand needle.

Insert the needle into both knit stitches from right to left, leave the purl stitch at the back.

Step 3

Insert the needle into the first purl stitch again from right to left, slip the first 2 stitches off the needle, pull the yarn through both stitches.

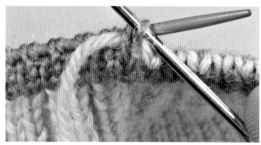

Insert the needle into the first purl stitch from right to left.

Repeat these steps until all stitches have been bound off.

Finished edge

Binding off the stitches

Cut the working yarn, leaving a tail about three times the circumference of the sock. Do not cut the yarn too short because you cannot join on another piece of yarn while you are binding off.
   When you are starting to bind off, the first stitch on the needle should be a purl stitch. If Needle 1 starts with a knit stitch, slip the last stitch of Needle 4 onto the left-hand needle.

SOCKS KNIT WITH CIRCULAR NEEDLES

Although many sock knitters prefer to work on double-pointed needles, there are others who want nothing to do with them. These knitters find that they work better with a circular needle than with double-pointed needles. Also, after working two or three pairs of socks on double-pointed needles, they sometimes find that although they can knit much faster, they have to stop constantly in order to change needles. After all, if you are working women's size 7/8 or men's size 5/6 socks, you will be changing needles about 700 times for each sock. Needle changes can also interrupt the flow when working patterns, or cause holes between the needles. And have you ever tried on a partly finished sock with the double-pointed needles still in it?

All these problems can be avoided by using circular needles instead of double-pointed needles. Plus, the knitting techniques you have learned are the same, and it is even possible to change from circular needles to double-pointed needles or vice versa at any time. It is certainly worth giving them a try!

Knitting with Two Circular Needles

Working on two circular needles makes knitting socks much faster. The flow of knitting is much smoother, and large pattern repeats are easier to knit.

Just remember that Needles 1 and 2 and Needles 3 and 4 are each joined by a flexible plastic cable. The stitches of two double-pointed needles are worked with the firm ends of just one circular needle; the second circular needle serves only to hold the other stitches in place. To allow more movement when knitting, slip the stitches not being worked onto the flexible center cable currently not in use.

Tip

The circular needles should be about 24"/60cm in length in order to work with them comfortably and not have too much of the flexible plastic cable in the way.

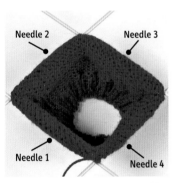

Stitches arranged evenly across 4 double-pointed needles

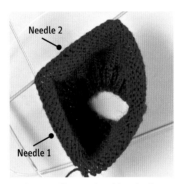

Replace Needles 3 and 4 with a circular needle.

Replace Needles 1 and 2 with a second circular needle.

HOW TO WORK

Cast on the required number of stitches evenly across 2 circular needles. Pull up the yarn firmly to tighten the stitches when changing from one needle to the other.

Stitches cast on evenly across 2 circular needles

Now carefully slip the stitches on Circular Needle 1 to the firm section of the needle, hold both needles together and parallel to each other, and turn. Do not let the cast-on row twist. To close the ring, knit the first stitch with the free end of the same needle, slip the stitches on the back needle to the flexible center cable of Circular Needle 2 (= the needle currently not in use), and slip the first stitch from Circular Needle 1.

While the stitches of the first row of the cuff are being knitted, the other half of the stitches are on the flexible cable of Circular Needle 2. Work the stitches on both parts of the needle in rib pattern with just one circular needle. Do not get the two circular needles mixed up!

At the end of the row, slip the stitches just worked onto the flexible center cable and leave them on one side.

While the stitches of the first round of the cuff are being worked with Circular Needle 2, the other half of the stitches are on one side on the flexible center cable of Circular Needle 1.

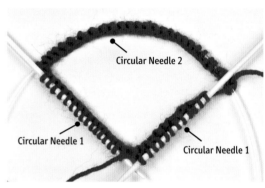

Slip the second half of the stitches of the first round of the cuff onto the firm section of Circular Needle 2 that is pointing toward the working yarn. Now work the stitches with the firm section of the same circular needle that is now empty. Once you reach the end of the row, slip the stitches you have just worked onto the flexible center cable and leave them on one side, turn.

While half of the stitches are being worked, the other half are "idle" on the flexible cable of the "idle" circular needle.

When changing from one circular needle to the other, all stitches are on the flexible center cable of the circular needles. This makes it easier to transport the knitting or to try on the sock for size.

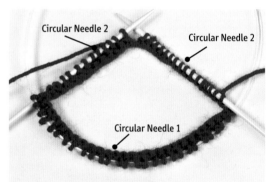

These instructions can be used to work entire socks. But make sure you don't get the needles mixed up. Each half of the stitches is always worked with only the two ends of a single circular needle; the second circular needle is left on one side. By keeping the two circular needles separated, many beginning sock knitters have no problems at all. If, however, the needles are constantly being interchanged, it might help to use circular needles made of different materials, e.g., steel, aluminum, bamboo, or hardwood. That way, if you work each half of the stitches with a different type of needle, you will quickly notice the difference, because the needles not only feel different but look different as well.

HEEL

The heel can easily be worked over the stitches on a circular needle. But in this case, you cannot use the yarn tail as a guide for the center of the heel. If you want to work the heel over the stitches on Circular Needles 4 and 1—in other words, with the yarn tail at the center—arrange the stitches on the circular needle so that the yarn tail is at the center of one of the two firm ends. But make sure that both firm ends still have the same number of stitches.

Knitting with One Circular Needle in Rounds
. . . knitting with a magic loop

Knitting in rounds with a magic loop and only one circular needle is a good alternative to double-pointed needles for those whose hands need a lot of space when knitting. In order to work comfortably, the circular needle should measure about 32"/80cm.

The magic loop—a loop at the center of the work—allows you to change direction at a place that is not at the end of one of the needles.

HOW TO WORK

Cast on all the stitches required on one circular needle. Slip the stitches onto the flexible center cable of the circular needle and pull up a loop from the cable at the center of the cast-on stitches between the stitches.

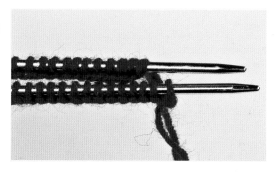

Slip both sections of the stitches back onto the firm end of the needle and hold both firm ends parallel. Do not let the cast-on edge twist. The working yarn is now attached to the last stitch on the back needle.

Move the back needle to the right and work the stitches on the front needle in rib pattern.

A loop is now protruding from either side of the rows of stitches on both the front and the back needles. Once all the stitches on one firm end have been worked, turn the work.

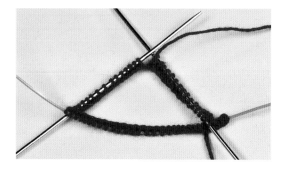

Slip the stitches of the front row onto the firm end. Move the back needle (= the end holding the stitches that have just been worked) to the right, work the stitches on the front needle, and turn. You can hold the loops that have formed on either together with the needles.

Repeat this last step over all the rounds and complete the sock. All the techniques described in this book can be worked this way.

HEEL

The heel can easily be worked over half of the stitches on a circular needle. But in this case, you cannot use the yarn tail as a guide for the center of the heel. If you want to work the heel with the yarn tail at the center, arrange the stitches on the circular needle with the use of double-pointed needles so that the working yarn is between the two needle points of the circular needle. Make sure that both sections of the circular needle have the same number of stitches.

Knitting Flat (Back and Forth) with One Circular Needle

Working socks flat can result in beautiful and yet unexpected pattern effects that would be very hard to achieve when working in rounds.

HALF A LEG WITH BEADED SELVAGE

Cast on half the stitches on a circular needle and work flat for the back of the leg down to the heel. It is important to work a beaded edge: knit the first and last stitch of every row (see page 41, "Double-Beaded Selvage").

LEG AND HEEL

Work the heel flat. If you decide to work the heel with additional rows, work 2 additional rows for the rounds. If you decide to work the heel with a gusset, work in rows, not rounds. Work the foot back and forth with a double-beaded selvage.

SHORT-ROW HEEL FOR TOES

A short-row heel for the toes provides the correct shape to join to the upper foot.

The short-row heel with reinforced double stitches, the wrap stitch heel, and the mock short-row heel are also suitable to use for shaping the toe area, because you can continue directly into the upper foot. All three types of heels also have stronger side seams, which make the toes more durable.

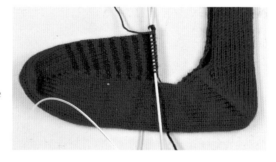

JOINING TO THE UPPER FOOT

While working the upper foot and the front leg, knit the last stitch of every row together with the next beaded stitch of the sole or the back leg to close open seams. Work the first stitch knitwise on right-side rows and purlwise on wrong-side rows.

PATTERNS

Hand-knit socks are a blessing for your feet; but more than that, they are real treasures that can be custom-made to suit the wearer. When hand-knit socks fit perfectly, there is a real sense of well-being, right down to the tips of the toes. Brightly colored and with beautiful patterns, these socks are really quick to make.

The patterns in this section are a good mixture of the various techniques shown in this book, with varying skill levels, so that you can put what you have learned into practice immediately.

- Uses basic knit and purl stitches in repetitive stitch patterns, including ribbing and simple lace.
- Uses more complex techniques, including lace, simple intarsia, and simple color changes.
- Involves intricate stitch patterns and techniques, such as cables, mosaics, and entrelac.

BABY'S SOCKS

... warm feet right from the start

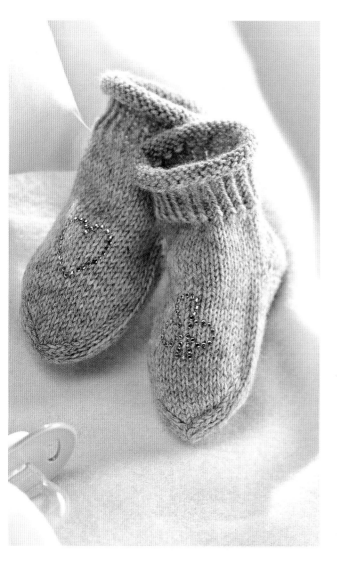

CUFF PATTERN
Rolled cuff with twisted 1 x 1 rib.

INSTRUCTIONS
Cast on 40 stitches. Work 8 rounds in stocki-nette stitch. Now work 8 rounds rib pattern for the cuff.

Work 10 rounds in stockinette stitch, then a short-row heel with reinforced double stitches, arranging the heel stitches 7/6/7. For the foot work 16 rounds in stockinette stitch. Decrease for the toe bands as follows: work to 3 stitches from the end of Needles 1 and 3, knit the next 2 stitches together; slip the second and third stitches on Needles 2 and 4 and knit both stit-ches together. After the first decrease round repeat the toe decreases on every second round twice more and on every round another 5 times. Cut the working yarn, pull the yarn through the remaining stitches to close, and weave in the yarn tail.

Iron on a rhinestone transfer letter onto the upper foot of each sock.

SKILL LEVEL

SIZE
- Infant's 3/4
- Continental 18/19

TECHNIQUES USED
- Thumb cast-on method (page 21)
- Rolled cuff (page 34)
- Twisted 1 x 1 rib cuff (page 29)
- Short-row heel with reinforced double stitches (page 56)
- Paired-decrease toes (page 71)

MATERIALS
- Wool-and-nylon blend fingering-weight yarn, such as Regia 4-ply (1/fingering; 75% wool, 25% nylon; each approx 1.8 oz/50g and 230 yrds/210m), Light Blue (#1945), one ball/50g
- five size 1–2/2–2.75mm double-pointed needles
- one embroidery or darning needle
- Rhinestone transfer letters (e.g., Gold-Zack from Prym)

GAUGE
30 stitches and 42 rounds in stockinette stitch = 4"/10cm

SKILL LEVEL

SIZE
- Women's 7/8
- Continental 38/39

TECHNIQUES USED
- Thumb cast-on method (page 21)
- Garter cuff (page 31)
- Short-row heel with reinforced double stitches (page 56)
- Spiral toes (page 75)

MATERIALS
- Silk-merino wool-nylon blend fingering-weight yarn, such as Regia Silk Color (1/fingering; 20% silk, 55% merino wool, 25% nylon; each approx. 1.8 oz/50g and 219 yrds/200m), Marokko Color (#0188), two balls/100g
- five size 1–2/2–2.75mm double-pointed needles
- one embroidery or darning needle

GAUGE
30 stitches and 42 rounds in basic pattern = 4"/10cm

GARTER WAVES
. . . self-patterning waves with lace patterns

CUFF PATTERN
Garter cuff

INSTRUCTIONS
Cast on 60 stitches and work 6 rounds in garter stitch for the cuff.

Continue, following the chart, working 2 pattern repeats each on 2 double-pointed needles and 1 more on a third needle. This avoids having to change needles in the middle of a pattern repeat. Work 7 pattern repeats in height, work the short-row heel with reinforced double stitches over the stitches on Needles 4 and 1, arranging the stitches 7/6/7. For the foot continue in rounds, working the stitches on Needles 2 and 3 in leg pattern, and the stitches on Needles 4 and 1 in stockinette stitch. When the work measures 7¾"/19.5cm from the center of the heel work the toe shaping.

Work the spiral in the toe shaping in the opposite direction for the other sock.

STITCH PATTERN FOR LEG AND UPPER FOOT
Best worked on 3 + 1 double-pointed needles
The stitches of all rounds are worked as they appear.

- ■ = K1
- — = P1
- ○ = yarn-over
- ▲ = K3 together slipped stitch over the three worked stitches

ENTIRELY NATURAL
...with textured pattern

STOCKINETTE STITCH
Knit right-side rows; purl wrong-side rows; knit all stitches in rounds

CUFF PATTERN
K1, then alternate P1, K2; end with P1, K1, following the chart below the broken line

BASIC PATTERN
On odd-numbered rounds work following the chart, repeat the motif of 6 stitches throughout. On even-numbered rounds work the stitches as they appear. Repeat rounds 1 to 8 throughout for pattern.

INSTRUCTIONS
Cast on 60 stitches and for the mini roll knit 3 rounds, then work ³/₄"/2cm in cuff pattern. Continue in basic pattern. When the leg measures about 5"/13cm work another ¹/₂"/1cm in stockinette stitch over the stitches on Needles 1 and 4, and in basic pattern over the stitches on Needles 2 and 3. Work the short-row heel in stockinette stitch, then work the foot. Work the heel. Continue in pattern as before the start of the heel. When the foot measures 7³/₄"/20cm work the toe shaping.

SKILL LEVEL

SIZE
- Women's 7/8
- Men's 5/6
- Continental 38/39

TECHNIQUES USED
- Thumb cast-on method (page 21)
- Short-row heel (page 56)
- Paired-decrease toes (page 71)

MATERIALS
- Wool-cotton-nylon blend fingering-weight yarn, such as Regia Cotton Color (1/fingering; 41% wool, 34% cotton, 25% nylon; each approx. 1.8/50g and 219 yrds/200m), Sienna Color (#5431), two balls/100g
- five size 2–3/1–3mm double-pointed needles
- one tapestry needle

GAUGE
30 stitches and 42 rounds in stockinette stitch = 4"/10cm

STITCH PATTERN

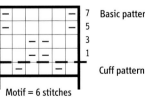

7 Basic pattern
5
3
1
Cuff pattern

Motif = 6 stitches

☐ = K1
⊟ = P1

SKILL LEVEL

SIZE

◆ Men's 10/11

◆ Continental 43/44

TECHNIQUES USED

◆ Reinforced thumb cast-on method (page 22)

◆ 2 x 2 rib cuff (page 29)

◆ Short-row heel with round shaping (page 57)

◆ Flower toes (page 76)

MATERIALS

◆ Wool-nylon-polyester blend fingering-weight yarn, such as Regia Stretch Color (1/fingering; 70% wool, 23% nylon, 7% polyester; each approx. 1.8/50g and 219 yrds/200m), Ottowa Color (#0122), two balls/100g

◆ five size 1/2.75mm double-pointed needles

◆ one blunt embroidery or darning needle

GAUGE

30 stitches and 42 rounds in basic pattern = 4"/10cm

CHEVRON SOCKS

... for men on the go

CUFF PATTERN

2 x 2 rib

INSTRUCTIONS

Cast on 64 stitches and work 20 rounds in cuff pattern. Continue in leg pattern following the chart, working motif 4 times total for height. Then work a short-row heel with round shaping over the 32 stitches on Needles 4 and 1 (stitch arrangement 10/9/10). Continue in rounds; work the stitches on Needles 2 and 3 in leg pattern, and those on Needles 4 and 1 in stockinette stitch.

When the work measures 9½"/23.5cm from center of heel, work the flower toe shaping.

STITCH PATTERN FOR LEG AND UPPER FOOT

■	= K1
—	= P1

FOR THE WELL-RESPECTED MAN

. . . and for the office too

STOCKINETTE STITCH
Knit right-side rows, purl wrong-side rows; knit all stitches in rounds

CUFF PATTERN
1 x 1 rib

TEXTURED PATTERN
Work each round following the chart above the broken line. Repeat the 8 stitches of the motif throughout.

Repeat rows 1 to 4 throughout for pattern.

INSTRUCTIONS
Cast on 64 stitches. and work ³/₄"/2cm in cuff pattern, then work 5"/13cm in textured pattern.

When the work measures 6"/13cm work another ¹/₂"/1cm in stockinette stitch over the stitches on Needles 1 and 4 and in textured pattern over the stitches on Needles 2 and 3.

Work a short-row heel, then continue in rounds for the foot: work the stitches on Needles 1 and 4 in stockinette stitch, and the stitches on Needles 2 and 3 in textured pattern. When the foot measures 8³/₄"/22cm work the toe shaping.

Work both socks alike.

SKILL LEVEL

SIZE
- Men's 9/10
- Continental 42/43

TECHNIQUES USED
- Thumb cast-on method (page 21)
- 1 x 1 rib cuff (page 29)
- Short-row heel (page 56)
- Paired-decrease toes (page 71)

MATERIALS
- Wool-and-nylon blend fingering-weight yarn, such as Regia 4-ply Color (1/fingering; 75% wool, 25% nylon; each approx 1.8 oz/50g and 230 yrds/210m), Patch Antic Sand (#5753), two balls/50g
- five size 1–3/2–3mm double-pointed needles
- one tapestry needle

GAUGE
30 stitches and 42 rounds in stockinette stitch = 4"/10cm

Note
Start each sock with the same color motif and take the yarn from the outside of the ball.

STITCH PATTERN

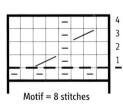

Textured pattern

Cuff pattern

Motif = 8 stitches

☐ = K1

— = P1

⬜⧄ = slip 1 onto a cable needle and leave at front of work, K1, then K1 from cable needle

SKILL LEVEL

SIZE

◆ Women's 13/14

◆ Men's 11/12

◆ Continental 44/45

TECHNIQUES USED

◆ Thumb cast-on method (page 21)

◆ 1 x 1 rib cuff (page 29)

◆ Short-row heel (page 56)

◆ Paired-decrease toes (page 71)

MATERIALS

◆ Wool-and-nylon blend fingering-weight yarn, such as Regia 6-ply (3/DK; 75% wool, 25% nylon; each approx 1.8 oz/50g and 137 yrds/125m), Mottled Gray-Blue (#1980), three balls/150g

◆ five size 3–6/3–4mm double-pointed needles

◆ one tapestry needle

GAUGE

22 stitches and 30 rounds in stockinette stitch = 4"/10cm

A TIMELESS CLASSIC

. . . with ribbed pattern

STOCKINETTE STITCH

Knit right-side rows; purl wrong-side rows; knit all stitches in rounds

CUFF PATTERN

Work each round following the chart below the broken line. Repeat the 7 stitches of the motif throughout. Repeat rounds 1 and 2 throughout for pattern.

RELIEF PATTERN

Work each round following the chart above the broken line. Repeat rounds 3 and 4 throughout for pattern.

INSTRUCTIONS

Cast on 56 stitches and work 1¼"/3cm in cuff pattern. Then continue in relief pattern.

When the work measures about 6"/15cm work another ½"/1cm in stockinette stitch over the stitches on Needles 1 and 4, and in relief pattern over the stitches on Needles 2 and 3.

Then work the heel and toes following basic pattern, working relief pattern over the front of the foot (Needles 2 and 3). When the foot measures 9"/23cm work the toes in stockinette stitch.

Work both socks alike.

STITCH PATTERN

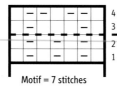

Motif = 7 stitches

Relief pattern

Cuff pattern

☐ = K1

⊟ = P1

FOR MOTHER AND DAUGHTER

... with lace pattern

SIZES

◆ Women's 5/6
Continental 36/37

◆ Children's 1-2
Continental 32/33

TECHNIQUES USED

◆ Thumb cast-on method
(page 21)

◆ Picot edging (page 33)

◆ Short-row heel
(page 52)

MATERIALS

◆ Wool-cotton-nylon
blend fingering-weight
yarn, such as Regia
Cotton (1/fingering;
41% wool, 34% cotton,
25% nylon; each
approx. 1.8/50g and
219 yrds/200m), White
(#0001), women's two
balls/100g; children's
one ball/50g

◆ five size 1–3/2–3mm
double-pointed
needles

◆ one size B/1–D/3/2–
3mm crochet hook

GAUGE

30 stitches and 42
rounds in stockinette
stitch = 4"/10cm

LACE PATTERN

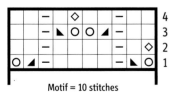

Motif = 10 stitches

☐ = K1

— = P1

○ = yarn-over

◣ = slip decrease knitwise over 2 sts
(= slip 1 knitwise, K1, pass slipped st over)

◢ = K2 together

Women's Socks

Knit right-side rows; purl wrong-side rows; knit all stitches in rounds

LACE PATTERN
Work all rounds in lace pattern following the chart. Repeat the motif of 10 stitches through-out. Repeat rounds 1 to 4 throughout for pattern.

INSTRUCTIONS
Cast on 60 stitches and for picot edging work 5 rounds in stockinette stitch. On the following round work alternately knit 2 together and yarn-over. Work another 5 rounds in stocki-nette stitch, and on the last round slip 1 stitch of the foundation edge onto the left-hand needle before each stitch and knit together with the next stitch on the needle.

Work 4"/10cm in lace pattern, then start the heel. Since the short-row heel is shorter than heels with heel flaps, work in stockinette stitch over the stitches on Needles 1 and 4, the first 2 stitches on Needle 2, and the last 2 stit-ches on Needle 3; work in lace pattern over the 26 center stitches on Needles 2 and 3. Work the heel and foot in basic pattern, continuing in pattern as before the start of the heel. When the foot measures 7¼"/18.5cm, work the toe shaping.

Work both socks alike.

Child's Socks

STOCKINETTE STITCH
Knit right-side rows; purl wrong-side rows; knit all stitches in rounds

LACE PATTERN
The number of stitches is a multiple of 4.
Round 1: *K2 together, yarn-over, K2, repeat from *.
Round 2: *K2, yarn-over, slip 1 stitch knitwise, K1, pass slipped stitch over, repeat from *.
Repeat rounds 1 and 2 throughout for pattern.

INSTRUCTIONS
Cast on 56 stitches. Knit one round, then conti-nue in lace pattern.

When work measures 3½"/9cm work ano-ther ½"/1cm in stockinette stitch over the stit-ches on Needles 1 and 4, continue in lace pat-tern over the stitches on Needles 2 and 3. Then work the foot.

Work the short-row heel in stockinette stitch, then continue in stockinette stitch over the stitches on Needles 1 and 4, and in lace pattern over the stitches on Needles 2 and 3 up to the toes. Work the toes in stockinette stitch.

Crochet picots around the foundation edge as follows: attach the working yarn at the cen-ter back with a chain stitch, then work *4 chain stitches, insert the hook back into the first chain stitch, and crochet 1 single crochet, skip 2 stitches of the previous row, slip 1 stitch *, repeat from * throughout.

Work both socks alike.

WAVY STRIPES
. . . the perfect start for a holiday

CUFF PATTERN
Garter cuff

INSTRUCTIONS

Cast on 70 stitches and work garter cuff over 6 rounds. Continue in pattern as follows: work 2 motifs over 28 stitches on Needle 1, and 1 motif over 14 stitches each on Needles 2, 3, and 4.

When work measures 6"/15cm from cast-on, work the heel as follows: on the first row knit another 4 stitches from Needle 2 with Needle 1. Knit the first stitch of the wrong-side row (= double-beaded selvage), and purl all remaining stitches. At the same time purl every eighth and ninth stitch together, then work another 3 stitches from Needle 4 with Needle 1, knit the last stitch again.

Continue over these 32 stitches for the heel. Continue in rounds for the foot: for the sole, work the stitches on Needles 1 and 4 in stockinette stitch, and for the upper foot, work the stitches on Needles 2 and 3 in pattern. So you do not work more decreases than increases, omit the first and last decrease and work the stitches in stockinette stitch.

When the work measures 7³/₄"/20cm from the center heel work all the stitches for the toes in stockinette stitch. Knit every eighth and ninth stitch on Needles 2 and 3, decreasing the number of stitches to 16 on each needle; end with star toe shaping.

Cut the working yarn, pull the yarn through the remaining 8 stitches to close, and weave in the yarn tail.

Work both socks alike.

SKILL LEVEL

SIZE
- Women's 7/8
- Men's 5/6
- Continental 38/39

TECHNIQUES USED
- Thumb cast-on method (page 21)
- Garter cuff (page 31)
- Right-slanting/left-slanting decreases (page 14)
- Round Heel (page 49)
- Star toes (page 73)

MATERIALS
- Wool-nylon-polyester blend fingering-weight yarn, such as Regia Stretch Color (1/fingering; 70% wool, 23% nylon, 7% polyester; each approx. 1.8/50g and 219 yrds/200m), Crazy Elektra (#0115), two balls/100g
- five size 1–2/ 2–2.75mm double-pointed needles
- one embroidery or darning needle

GAUGE
35 stitches and 40 rows in basic pattern = 4"/10cm

STITCH PATTERN FOR LEG AND UPPER FOOT

◆	■	■	■	■	—	◆	—	■	■	■	■	◆	◆		2
○	■	■	■	◣	—	◆	—	◢	■	■	■	○	◆		1

- ■ = K1
- — = P1
- ◆ = K1 through back of loop
- ○ = yarn-over
- ◢ = K2 together
- ◣ = slip 2 stitches and knit together

SIZE
◆ Women's 7/8
◆ Men's 5/6
◆ Continental 38/39

TECHNIQUES USED
◆ Thumb cast-on method (page 21)
◆ Twisted 1 x 1 rib cuff (page 29)
◆ Horseshoe heel (page 45)
◆ Right- and left-slanting decreases (page 14)
◆ Anatomically shaped toes (page 73)
◆ Paired-decrease toe (page 71)
◆ Kitchener stitch (page 15)

MATERIALS
◆ Bamboo-wool-nylon blend fingering-weight yarn, such as Regia Bamboo Color (1/fingering; 45% bamboo, 40% wool, 15% nylon; each approx. 1.8/50g and 219 yrds/200m), Jamaica Color (#1066), two balls/100g
◆ five size 0–5/2–2.75mm double-pointed needles
◆ one tapestry needle

GAUGE
30 stitches and 42 rows in basic pattern = 4"/10cm

ANATOMICAL SOCKS
This attractive design provides plenty of extra toe room.

STITCH PATTERN

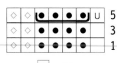

● = K1
◇ = P1
U = yarn over
☐ = empty boxes are construction markers only, ignore

●●●● = slip 1, K3, pass slipped stitch over the three worked stitches

CUFF PATTERN
Twisted 1 x 1 rib

INSTRUCTIONS
Cast on 60 stitches. Purl one round, then work 16 rounds in rib pattern. Continue in stitch pattern (work motif 10 times) until the work measures 7" (approx. 17¾cm) from the cast-on edge. For an easy transition to the heel, end with a fifth row in pattern. Work the heel over the stitches on Needles 4 and 1 as follows: on the first row of the heel flap, work 2 more stitches on Needle 1 from Needle 2; on the first wrong-side row of the heel flap, slip the last 2 stitches on Needle 4 unworked onto Needle 3, then turn and work over these 30 stitches for the heel flap.

For the horseshoe heel, knit 18 stitches, work 1 double stitch, turn. Slip 1 stitch, purl 6 stitches, work 1 double stitch, turn. Repeat the short rows until there are just 7 stitches on both sides. On all following rounds work the last stitch of the center panel together with the first stitch of the side panel until all side panel stitches have been used up.

Continue in rounds. Pick up 15 new stitches along each side edge of each heel flap, then with Needle 2 pick up 1 more stitch through the back of the horizontal strand between Needles 1 and 2, purl this stitch. Work all remaining stitches on Needles 2 and 3 in pattern.

Work as many gusset decreases as required until there are 15 stitches on each heel needle again.

Work the foot even until it measures 8"/20.5cm from the center of the heel, keeping the pattern arrangements correct (15 + 16 + 15 + 15). Work all the stitches on the last round before starting the toes knitwise, and at the same time slip the second and third stitches on Needle 2 and knit both stitches together (left slanting).

RIGHT SOCK
Work anatomical banded toes until 6 stitches remain on each needle. Close the stitches as for a double-decrease band.

LEFT SOCK
Knit the left sock in reverse, working the banded toe decreases first just over the stitches on Needles 3 and 4, then later including the decreases over Needles 1 and 2.

RIBS AND CABLES

These slender cables extend down into the heel at the back, and into the top of the foot as ribbing.

CUFF PATTERN
Twisted garter cuff

INSTRUCTIONS
Cast on 64 stitches and work a twisted garter cuff. Arrange stitches evenly across 4 double-pointed needles and join to a round.

Continue in leg pattern following the chart, working the entire motif of 14 rounds 3 times.

For the heel flap, work 30 rows in the stitch pattern over the stitches on Needles 4 and 1, with a garter selvage stitch on either end of each row.

Work heart-shaped heel onto the patterned heel flap. Continue again in rounds, picking up stitches along the garter selvage and gusset decreases; work in stockinette stitch over the stitches on Needles 4 and 1, and row 1 of pattern over the stitches on Needles 2 and 3.

When work measures 8¹/₂"/21.5cm from the center of the heel, work the toes in stockinette stitch.

For the paired toe decreases, work to 3 stitches from the end of Needles 1 and 3 and knit the next 2 stitches together (left-slanting decrease), knit 1;, knit the second and third stitches on Needles 2 and 4 together. Repeat these decreases on every fourth round once, on every third round twice, on every second round 3 times, and on every round 7 times. Cut the working yarn, pull it through the remaining 8 stitches to close, and weave in the yarn end. Close the first rows of the twisted garter cuff with the working yarn.

Work both socks alike.

SKILL LEVEL

SIZE
◆ Women's 9/10
◆ Men's 7/8
◆ Continental 40/41

TECHNIQUES USED
◆ Thumb cast-on method (page 21)
◆ Twisted garter cuff (page 31)
◆ Heart-shaped heel (page 48)
◆ Banded toes (page 65)

MATERIALS
◆ Wool-and-nylon blend fingering-weight yarn, such as Regia 4-ply (1/fingering; 75% wool, 25% nylon; each approx 1.8 oz/50g and 230 yrds/210m), Red Wine (#1036), two balls/50g
◆ five size 0–5/2–2.75mm double-pointed needles
◆ one tapestry needle

GAUGE
30 stitches and 42 rows in basic pattern = 4"/10cm

STITCH PATTERN FOR LEG, UPPER FOOT, AND HEEL FLAP

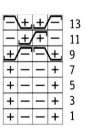

Work stitches on even rounds and rows as they appear.

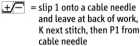

+ = K1

− = P1

+/+ = slip 1 onto a cable needle and leave at back of work, K next stitch, then K1 from cable needle

+/− = slip 1 onto a cable needle and leave at back of work, K next stitch, then P1 from cable needle

−\+ = slip 1 onto a cable needle and leave at front of work, P next stitch, then K1 from cable needle

SIZE

- Women's 7/8
- Men's 5/6
- Continental 38/39

TECHNIQUES USED

- Thumb cast-on method (page 21)
- Paired-decrease toes bands (page 71)

MATERIALS

- Wool-nylon-polyester blend fingering-weight yarn, such as Regia Stretch (1/fingering; 70% wool, 23% nylon, 7% polyester; each approx. 1.8/50g and 219 yrds/200m), White (#0001), one ball/50g

- Wool-nylon-polyester blend fingering-weight yarn, such as Regia Stretch (1/fingering; 70% wool, 23% nylon, 7% polyester; each approx. 1.8/50g and 219 yrds/200m), Black (#0099), one ball/50g

- Wool-and-nylon blend fingering-weight yarn, such as Regia 4-ply (1/fingering; 75% wool, 25% nylon; each approx 1.8 oz/50g and 230 yrds/210m), Raspberry (#1258), one ball/50g

- Five size 1–3/2–3mm double-pointed needles

- one size D/3–F/5/ 3–3.5mm crochet hook

- one embroidery or darning needle

GAUGE

30 stitches and 42 rounds in stockinette stitch = 4"/10cm

SPORT SOCKS

... sockettes for sneakers

STOCKINETTE STITCH

Knit right-side rows; purl wrong-side rows; knit all stitches in rounds

TWO-COLOR HALF FISHERMAN'S RIB

Work over an even number of stitches.

Round 1, Black: knit all stitches.

Round 2, White: purl all stitches.

Round 3, Black: *P1, then insert the needle into the next stitch of the row below and K1, repeat from *.

Work round 1 once, then repeat rounds 2 and 3 throughout for pattern.

INSTRUCTIONS

Cast on 60 stitches with Raspberry and knit 3 rounds. Work 15 rounds (= 1"/2.5cm) in two-color half fisherman's rib, then knit one round in Black. Continue in stockinette stitch for 2 rounds with Raspberry, then work the heel with White in the method of your choice. Continue in rounds, working alternately 6 rounds with Black, 2 rounds with Raspberry. When the foot measures 7¾"/20cm work the toes with White. Work a crocheted chain with 10 chain stitches at the center back of the cast-on edge with the double yarn.

Work both sockettes alike.

SOCKS FOR SHOPPING

... with cord

STOCKINETTE STITCH
Knit right-side rows; purl wrong-side rows; knit all stitches in rounds

CUFF PATTERN
2 x 2 rib

INSTRUCTIONS
For the right sock loosely cast on 60 stitches with Mottled Mid Gray and for the double cuff work in stockinette stitch.

After 12 rounds work the stitches on Needle 1, then work 3 rows between the stitches on Needles 1 and 2 for the front slit, then continue again in rounds. After 18 rounds (= about 1³/₄"/4.5cm) knit 1 stitch on each needle and 1 stitch on the foundation edge together.

Then continue in stockinette stitch with Jacquard Paris, increasing 12 stitches evenly across the first round (= 72 stitches). When the work measures about 5"/13cm from the double cuff decrease these 12 stitches again evenly across, continue with Mottled Mid Gray. Work the first round in stockinette stitch, then work 10 rounds in cuff pattern. Work another ¹/₂"/1cm in stockinette stitch, then work the heel and foot.

Work the left sock in reverse (= work the slit in the double cuff between Needles 3 and 4).

Make two cords with Mottled Mid Gray, each about 16"/40cm long. Feed the cords through the cuff with a safety pin, secure each end with a stopper (see photograph).

SKILL LEVEL

SIZE
- Women's 7/8
- Men's 5/6
- Continental 38/39

TECHNIQUES USED
- Thumb cast-on method (page 21)
- 2 x 2 rib cuff (page 29)
- Short-row heel (page 56)
- Paired-decrease toes (page 71)

MATERIALS
- Wool-and-nylon blend fingering-weight yarn, such as Regia 4-ply (1/fingering; 75% wool, 25% nylon; each approx 1.8 oz/50g and 230 yrds/210m), Jacquard Paris (#5295), two balls/100g
- Wool-and-nylon blend fingering-weight yarn, such as Regia 4-ply (1/fingering; 75% wool, 25% nylon; each approx 1.8 oz/50g and 230 yrds/210m), Mottled Mid Gray (#0044), one ball/50g
- five size 1–3/2–3mm double-pointed needles
- one safety pin
- two antique silver cord stoppers
- one tapestry needle

GAUGE
30 stitches and 42 rounds in stockinette stitch = 4"/10cm

Tip:

Start both socks with the same color motif, taking the yarn from the outside of the ball.

SIZE

- Men's 9/10
- Continental 42/43

TECHNIQUES USED

- Thumb cast-on method (page 21)
- 2 x 2 rib cuff (page 29)
- Paired-decrease toes (page 71)
- Right- and left-slanting decreases (page 14)
- Peasant heel with waste yarn (page 67)
  Pulling stitches together to close (page 64)

MATERIALS

- Wool-and-nylon blend fingering-weight yarn, such as Regia 4-ply Color (1/fingering; 75% wool, 25% nylon; each approx 1.8 oz/50g and 230 yrds/210m), Sylt (#5030), one ball/50g
- Wool-and-nylon blend fingering-weight yarn, such as Regia 4-ply (1/fingering; 75% wool, 25% nylon; each approx 1.8 oz/50g and 230 yrds/210m), Royal blue (#2000), two balls/100g
- five size 1–2/2–2.75mm double-pointed needles
- one blunt embroidery needle

GAUGE

30 stitches and 42 rounds in basic pattern = 4"/10cm

MOSAIC PATTERN

... for men

STITCH PATTERN FOR LEG AND UPPER FOOT

■	U	■	U	■	■	■	■	■	U	27
U	■	U	■	U	■	■	■	■	■	25
■	U	■	U	■	U	■	■	■	■	23
■	■	U	■	U	■	U	■	■	■	21
■	■	■	U	■	U	■	U	■	■	19
■	■	■	■	U	■	U	■	U	■	17
■	■	■	■	■	U	■	U	■	U	15
U	■	■	■	■	■	U	■	U	■	13
■	U	■	■	■	■	■	U	■	U	11
U	■	U	■	■	■	■	■	U	■	9
■	U	■	U	■	■	■	■	■	U	7
U	■	U	■	U	■	■	■	■	■	5
■	■	U	■	U	■	U	■	■	■	3
■	■	■	■	U	U	■	U	■	■	1

← Start

■ = K1

U = slip 1 stitch, yarn at back of work

Work pale gray-shaded rounds plus 1 more round with Royal Blue; work white-shaded rounds plus 1 more round with Sylt Color. Twist the yarn together at the end of every round to avoid holes from forming.

CUFF PATTERN

2 x 2 rib

INSTRUCTIONS

Cast on 64 stitches with Royal Blue and work 1 ¼"/3cm in 2 x 2 rib.

Change to mosaic pattern. With Sylt work one round in stockinette stitch, and at the same time pick up 1 stitch through the back of the horizontal strand between Needles 1 and 2 with Needle 2, and pick up 1 stitch between Needles 2 and 3 with Needle 3 (16 + 17 + 17 + 16).

In order for the pattern on the upper foot to look symmetrical, work the stitches on Needle 1 with Sylt once more. Now work mosaic pattern following the chart (= work motif 6 times), starting with Needle 2 at the stitch marker. The round change is now between Needles 1 and 2. Twist the yarn together at the end of every round.

When the work measures about 7"/18 cm from the cuff, work the heel.

First separate the yarns. With waste yarn work over the 32 stitches on Needles 4 and 1. Attach the Royal Blue yarn to Needle 1 and continue in rounds. The round change is now at the center of the heel and sole between Needles 4 and 1, as usual. Work the stitches of the upper foot over Needles 2 and 3 in pattern, and the stitches for the sole on Needles 1 and 4 in stockinette stitch. Work 2 rounds with Royal Blue and 2 rounds with Sylt.

When the work measures 7"/17.5cm from the waste yarn, with Royal Blue work one round in stockinette stitch over all the stitches, work the toe bands.

Carefully remove the waste yarn and arrange all the stitches evenly across 4 double-pointed needles. From the center of the sole count out 16 + 17 + 17 + 16 stitches on the needles. With Royal Blue work 2 rounds in stockinette stitch over all the stitches. Work the peasant heel. Cut the working yarn, pull it through the remaining 8 stitches to close, and weave in the yarn tail.

Work both socks alike.

FOLKLORE SOCKS
. . . with cables

SKILL LEVEL

SIZE
- Women's 7/8
- Men's 5/6
- Continental 38/39

TECHNIQUES USED
- Thumb cast-on method (page 21)
- Short-row heel (page 56)
- Paired-decrease toes (page 71)

MATERIALS
- Wool-and-nylon blend fingering-weight yarn, such as Regia Tweed 4-ply (1/fingering; 75% wool, 25% nylon; each approx 1.8 oz/50g and 230 yrds/210m), Ecru Tweed (#0002), two balls/100g
- five size 1–3/2–3mm double-pointed needles
- one embroidery or darning needle

GAUGE
30 stitches and 42 rounds in stockinette stitch = 4"/10cm

STOCKINETTE STITCH
Knit right-side rows; purl wrong-side rows; in rounds knit all stitches.

CUFF PATTERN
1 x 1 rib, following the chart below the broken line

BASIC PATTERN
Work odd-numbered rounds following the chart above the broken line, repeat motif of 16 stitches throughout. On even-numbered rounds work stitches as they appear or as indicated in the chart. Repeat rounds 1 to 8 throughout for pattern.

INSTRUCTIONS
Cast on 64 stitches and work 3¼"/8cm in cuff pattern. Continue in basic pattern.

When the leg measures 7¾"/20cm slip 4 stitches from each needle onto the previous needle, then continue in stockinette stitch over the stitches on Needles 1 and 4, knit 2 stitches together twice on the first round (= 15 stitches each on Needles 1 and 4). Work in stockinette stitch over the first 3 stitches on Needle 2 and the last 4 stitches on Needle 3, and in basic pattern over the 25 stitches in between. After another 4 rounds work the foot and heel. Work the stitches on Needles 1 and 4 in stockinette stitch, and those on Needles 2 and 3 in basic pattern as before.

When the foot measures about 7¾"/20cm knit one round, knit 2 stitches together once each over Needles 2 and 3 (= 15 stitches on each needle), then work the toes in stockinette stitch.

Work both socks alike.

BASIC PATTERN

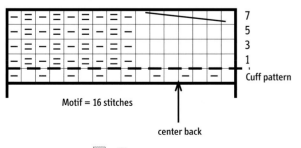

7
5
3
1

Cuff pattern

Motif = 16 stitches

center back

☐ = K1

⊟ = P1

⊟ = on odd rounds slip 1 purlwise with yarn-over; on even rounds K1 tog with the yarn-over

|4| |3| = slip 4 onto a cable needle and leave at front of work, K3, then K4 from cable needle

SIZE

- Women's 7/8
- Men's 5/6
- Continental 38/39

TECHNIQUES USED

- Thumb cast-on method (page 21)
- Twisted 2 x 2 rib cuff (page 29)
- Right- and left-slanting decreases (page 14)
- Wrap stitches (page 58)
- Peasant heel (page 67)
- Paired-decrease toes (page 71)
- Kitchener stitch (page 15)

MATERIALS

- Silk-merino wool-nylon blend fingering-weight yarn, such as Regia Silk Color (1/fingering; 20% silk, 55% merino wool, 25% nylon; each approx. 1.8 oz/50g and 219 yrds/200m), Ocean Color (#0191), two balls/100g
- five size 1–2/ 2–2.75mm double-pointed needles
- one embroidery or darning needle

GAUGE

30 stitches and 42 rounds in basic pattern = 4"/10cm

BASKET WEAVE SOCKS

... woven, knitted, and sewn together

CUFF PATTERN
Twisted 2 x 2 rib

BASIC PATTERN
Entrelac and basket weave technique with striped yarn

INSTRUCTIONS
Cast on 60 stitches and arrange them evenly across 4 double-pointed needles.

Work 20 rounds in cuff pattern. Work the following round in stockinette stitch, and at the same time knit every fifth stitch together with the following stitch. There are now 50 stitches on the double-pointed needles.

Starting triangles (left slanting)
The starting triangles are now worked in open rows. Slip the first stitch of each row.

Knit 2 stitches, turn.
Slip 1 stitch, purl 1 stitch, turn.
Slip 1 stitch, knit 2 stitches, turn.

Continue in pattern, taking 1 stitch more into the row from the cuff at the end of every right-side row until there are 5 knit stitches on the needle.

Do not turn, but join on the next triangle starting with 2 knit stitches until there are 10 starting triangles.

Turn the work once more to change to the round with right-slanting rectangles, slip 1 stitch, and purl 4 stitches.

Right-slanting rectangles
Pick up 5 stitches purlwise along the side of the downwards-slanting edge of the rectangle adjacent to the stitches, turn.

Slip 1 stitch, knit 4 stitches, turn.
Slip 1 stitch, purl 3 stitches, purl the last picked-up stitch together with the first stitch of the next triangle or rectangle. Turn, slip 1 stitch, knit 4 stitches, turn.

Continue in pattern, and purl the last stitch of the just-worked rectangle together with the first stitch of a triangle or rectangle at the end of a wrong-side row below until all 5 stitches have been used up. Do not turn, but join on the next right-slanting rectangle by again picking up 5 stitches purlwise along the edge of the adjacent triangle. Work a round with 10 right-slanting rectangles.

To change to a round with left-slanting rectangles, turn the work once more, slip 1 stitch, and knit 4 stitches.

Left-slanting rectangles

Pick up 5 stitches knitwise along the side of the upwards-slanting edge of the rectangle adjacent to the stitches on the needle, turn, slip 1 stitch, purl 4 stitches, turn.

Slip 1 stitch, knit 3 stitches; to decrease, slip the last picked-up stitch knitwise together with the first stitch of the rectangle on the row below, slip both stitches back onto the left-hand needle, and knit them together.

Turn, slip 1 stitch, purl 4 stitches, turn. Now work the rectangle over these stitches by slipping the last stitch of every right-side row together with the first stitch of the rectangle of the row below and knitting both stitches together until all 5 stitches have been used up.

Do not turn, but join on the next left-slanting rectangle by again picking up 5 stitches knitwise along the side edge of the next triangle. Work a round with 10 left-slanting rectangles the same way.

To change to a round with right-slanting rectangles, turn the work once more, slip 1 stitch, and purl 4 stitches.

Work 11 rounds of alternate right-slanting and left-slanting rectangles, end the leg with right-slanting rectangles.

Final triangles (left slanting)

Again pick up 5 stitches knitwise along the side of the upwards-slanting edge of the rectangle of the row below, turn, and slip 1 stitch, purl 4 stitches, turn.

Slip 1 stitch, knit 3 stitches, slip the last picked-up stitch and the first stitch of the rectangle of the row below and knit them together (left slanting). Turn the work, slip 1 stitch, purl 3 stitches, work 1 wrap stitch (= slip the stitch onto the right-hand needle without working it, bringing the yarn around the stitch from the front to the back), turn.

Work the final triangle by slipping the last stitch of every right-side row together with the first stitch of every rectangle of the previous row and knitting them together. At at the end of every wrong-side row work 1 stitch less, slipping this as a wrap stitch instead. The wrap stitches of the previous rows are not worked, but are left on the left-hand needle.

When all 5 stitches are on the needle as wrap stitches, do not turn, but join on the next left-slanting final triangle by picking up 5 stitches knitwise along the side edge of the adjacent triangle. Work a row of 10 final triangles.

There are now 50 stitches on the needles. On the following round knit all the stitches, and at the same time knit each stitch and its respective wrap stitch together (see page 58, "Working Wrap Stitches").

At the end of every final triangle (= after every 5 stitches) pick up 1 additional stitch through the back of the horizontal strand between two triangles. There are now 60 stitches on the needles. Knit one round, working the stitches on Needles 4 and 1 with waste yarn. Reattach the working yarn to Needle 4 and continue with the foot as if the heel had already been completed. Work the entire foot in stockinette stitch until it measures 6"/15cm from the waste yarn.

For the toe shaping, work to 3 stitches from the ends of Needles 1 and 3 and knit 2 stitches together; slip the second and third stitches on Needles 2 and 4 and knit both stitches together (left slanting). Repeat these decreases on the fourth round once, on every third round twice, on every second round 3 times, and on every round 6 times until just the 8 band stitches remain. Cut the working yarn, pull the yarn through the remaining 8 stitches to close, and weave in the yarn tail.

Remove the waste yarn, pick up all 60 stitches, and arrange them evenly across 4 double-pointed needles. The round starts at the center of the lower heel. Work 1 more round in stockinette stitch, then work the upper toe decreases for the peasant heel. Repeat these decreases on the fourth round once, on every third round twice, on every second round 3 times and on the following round once without any additional rounds until just 7 stitches remain on each needle. Without any additional rows, work 1 additional round with Kitchener stitch: knit the last 2 stitches on Needles 1 and 3 together; slip the first 2 stitches on Needle 2, and knit both stitches together left slanting. Knit the 6 stitches on Needle 1 once more, then close all stitches using Kitchener stitch.

Weave in all yarn tails.

TRANSFERRING PATTERNS

There are a large number of patterns for knitting socks flat (back and forth), and almost all of these patterns can be converted to knitting in rounds. Doing this also encourages you to develop your own designs.

Notation of Knitting Patterns

When patterns are written out fully, you read the instructions for right-side and wrong-side rows as text—from left to right and from top to bottom. Pattern repeats and motifs are usually indicated by means of symbols. Some knitting patterns can be unwieldy and long. Many abbreviations make patterns with a larger repeat confusing. Perhaps that is why German patterns tend to have charts, while English patterns are worked by following written-out instructions. Frequently you don't actually get a "feel" for the pattern until you have worked several rows, and mistakes are only identified at the ends of the rows, when you have either too many or too few stitches.

Following is an example of a written-out pattern. It is of the anatomical toe shaping instructions found on page 106.

> **Rows 1, 3, 7, and 9** (right-side rows): Selvage stitch, *P2, K4 *, P2, selvage stitch.
>
> **Rows 2, 4, 6, and 8** (wrong-side rows): Selvage stitch, K2, *P4, K2 *, selvage stitch.
>
> **Row 5**: selvage stitch, *P2, yarn-over, slip 1, K3, pass slipped stitch over the 3 worked stitches *, P2, selvage stitch.
>
> **Row 10**: selvage stitch, P2, *P3, slip the 3 stitches back onto the left-hand needle, pass the 4th stitch over, slip the 3 stitches back onto the right-hand needle *, selvage stitch.

In comparison, charts allow you to visualize the patterns more easily. Symbols of all the stitches that are found in the pattern, such as yarn-overs or bobbles, are listed in a key and appear just as they are in the pattern. You read the right-side rows of the charts as you knit them, in other words from right to left and from bottom to top. Wrong-side rows are given in the opposite direction since you change direction when you turn the knitting. In this way the stitches of the chart appear exactly where they will appear in the pattern. Frequently, a brief glance at the chart can show exactly what the pattern will look like when complete. The row numbers mark the start of each row; for right-side rows these are on the right side of the chart, for wrong-side rows they are on the left side.

The above description shown as a chart:

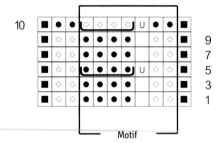

Motif

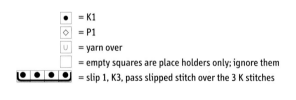

- ● = K1
- ◇ = P1
- U = yarn over
- ☐ = empty squares are place holders only; ignore them
- |●|●|●|●| = slip 1, K3, pass slipped stitch over the 3 K stitches

Transferring Written-out Patterns to Charts

PREPARING THE GRAPH PAPER

First, look just at the pattern repeat—in other words, just at that part of the pattern that is marked to be repeated between the stars, asterisks, or parentheses. Make a note of the number of stitches and rows. In our example, this is 6 stitches (= 2 purl stitches, 4 knit stitches) and 10 rows.

Mark this pattern repeat at the center of your graph paper, and draw two vertical lines, one on either side, marking out the number of squares needed for the pattern repeat. The vertical lines should also mark the number of rows required by the repeat.

COPYING THE STITCHES AND STITCH ELEMENTS

Now assign signs or symbols to all stitches and stitch elements and make a note of these symbols in a small chart. Small geometric symbols are ideal for this, either filled-in or as outlines, for example.

Now fill in the bottom row between the two vertical lines using the symbols to stand for the written-out pattern. Read from left to right, but write from right to left! Transfer all the other right-side rows to the chart, leaving one row of squares empty in between for the wrong-side rows, which will be added later.

Then transfer the final stitches and the selvage stitches of all the right-side rows to the chart and enter the row numbers along the right edge.

Next, enter the motif for the wrong-side rows. As before, read the written-out wrong-side rows from left to right, and enter them on the chart from left to right. By turning the work you change the direction of your knitting, and the stitches are worked in reverse order to the right-side row. Finally, transfer all wrong-side rows to the empty rows of squares, then add the ends of the patterns, the selvage stitches on either side of the vertical lines, and the row numbers of the wrong-side rows along the left edge.

REDUCING THE NUMBER OF ROWS

Sometimes patterns require additional rows as wrong-side rows. These wrong-side rows require all stitches to be worked as they appear, so that a knit stitch on a right-side row would be purled on a wrong-side row, and a purl stitch on a right-side row would become a knit stitch on a wrong-side row. All stitch elements are purled on wrong-side rows.

Exceptions to the above are given in the key, as in the following example:

N = work 1 bobble, knit wrong-side row

◆ = knit 1 stitch through back of loop, purl through back of loop on all wrong-side rows

Since wrong-side rows don't usually provide any additional information, they are only given in the chart if a pattern is worked on this row, as with row 10 of our example. By leaving out these additional rows, charts become easier to read. For example, if you use a light-colored symbol for all knit stitches and a dark-colored symbol for all purl stitches, you will get a good idea of what the final pattern will look like from the chart alone.

Now look at the chart you have produced and check to see if the right-side rows are worked only as additional rows or if they contain stitches relating to the pattern. All additional rows can be removed, leaving the wrong-side rows—those rows with the stitch elements for the pattern—in place.

If you want to use the chart for working with rows, copy the chart neatly, and start knitting.

Please note that there is one additional step needed when working in rounds.

Making Rows into Rounds

If patterns are being worked in rows, you need to give some thought to how to finish the round at the end of the pattern repeat. This problem does not arise when working in rounds since there are no edges. A pattern repeat for rows is easy to convert into one for rounds for the simple reason that only the pattern repeat is actually repeated. Initial stitches, final stitches, and selvage stitches are not needed when working in the round. The advantage of leaving out the additional rows when working in rounds is that it makes no difference which direction the additional rows are being worked in. Whether they are worked on wrong-side rows, in the opposite direction to the direction of working a patterned right-side row, or as another right-side row when working rounds, nothing will change regarding the stitch layout. The stitches of the additional rows are worked as they appear—even when working in rounds.

If you now copy the chart neatly, you just need to check whether, as in our example, a patterned wrong-side row has to be converted into a right-side row for the purpose of working in the round (this is not an additional row but rather a row that changes the appearance of the pattern). Knit stitches will have to be written as purl stitches and purl stitches as knit stitches; cables and slipped decreases have to be worked in the opposite direction.

Our example repeated:

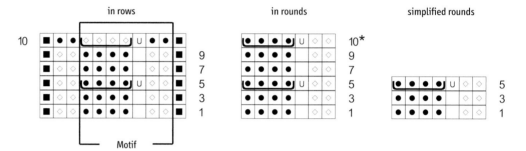

in rows   in rounds   simplified rounds

Marking round 10 with a star or an asterisk as a reminder that no additional rounds are to be worked after round 9 but rather a patterned round.

It is now possible to simplify our sample chart even more.

What Else Is There to Consider?

In principle, any pattern can be worked on the leg. However, it is very important that you always work a gauge swatch, as patterns frequently behave differently than when worked in plain stockinette stitch. If a pattern requires a different number of stitches than is given for the cuff, foot, or sole, this can easily be amended. Work over the patterned part with a different number of stitches, adjusting the change-over to the pattern by increasing or decreasing stitches.

The change-over to the upper foot is sometimes a bit difficult if the pattern requires an additional stitch in order for the pattern to be symmetrical when changing to the sole. In this case, pick up 1 additional stitch through the back of the horizontal strand between the heel and the sole in the appropriate position at the end of the heel. This stitch can be reduced again by an additional decrease in the toes later.

If the pattern repeat has an even number of stitches, thought should be given to the appearance of the pattern on the upper foot, even before starting the heel, since in this case half a motif will always be visible on either side. Some patterns are well-balanced as they are; but for others, it is better to position the patterns at the center of the upper foot and to end the patterns on either side, as if you were working in rows. The heel can then be moved by a half or quarter of a motif by moving the double-pointed needles by the respective number of stitches to one side.

On the other hand, an empty piece of graph paper is also an invitation to design your own pattern once you have written down the number of stitches needed for the upper foot. For the leg, just work double the number of stitches as are needed for the upper foot.

Have fun experimenting!

YARN WEIGHT CATEGORIES	TYPES OF YARN IN CATEGORY	KNIT GAUGE RANGE (ST ST TO 4 INCHES)	RECOMMENDED NEEDLE SIZES
0 LACE	Fingering 10-count crochet thread	30–34 sts	#000–1/1.5–2.25mm
1 SUPER FINE	Lace, fingering, baby	27–32 sts	#1–3/2.25–3.25mm
2 FINE	Sport, baby	23–26 sts	#3–5/3.25–3.75mm
3 LIGHT	DK, light worsted	21–24 sts	#5–7/3.75–4.5mm
4 MEDIUM	Worsted, afghan, aran	16–20 sts	#7–9/4.5–5.5mm
5 BULKY	Chunky, craft, rug	12–15 sts	#9–11/5.5–8mm
6 SUPER BULKY	Bulky, roving	6–11 sts	#11 and larger/8mm and larger

Adapted from the Standard Yarn Weight System of the Craft Yarn Council of America.

The patterns in this book were each designed with a specific yarn in mind. If you substitute a recommended yarn, you should choose one with the same weight and a similar fiber content. You should always take time to make a gauge swatch before you begin a pattern, but it's especially important to do so if you are substituting the suggested yarn. If necessary, change needle sizes to obtain the correct gauge.

HEEL SIZES WITH FINGERING-WEIGHT OR 4-PLY SOCK YARN

1¾ oz/50g, 229 yards/210m, 30 stitches x 42 rows = 4"/10cm

Children's and women's sizes	5/5½	6/7	8/9	9½/10	11/11½	12/13	1/2	3/4	5/6	7/8	9/9½	10/11	12/13	14/15
Men's sizes									5/6	7/8	7/8	9/10	11/12	13/14
Continental sizes	20/21/	22/23	24/25	26/27	28/29	30/31	32/33	34/35	36/37	38/39	40/41	42/43	44/45	46/47
Stitches (total)	44	44	48	48	52	52	56	56	60	60	64	64	68	72
Stitches per needle	11	11	12	12	13	13	14	14	15	15	16	16	17	18
Heel stitches	22	22	24	24	26	26	28	28	30	30	32	32	34	36
HEEL FLAP STITCHES: HEEL FLAP, HORSESHOE, HEART, AND ROUND HEELS														
Heel height, rows	22	22	24	24	26	26	28	28	30	30	32	32	34	36
Stitches, gusset	7/8/7		8/8/8		9/8/9		9/10/9		10/10/10		10/12/10		11/12/11	12/12/12
Stitches, horseshoe	5/6/6/5		6/6/6/6		7/6/6/7		8/6/6/8		7/8/8/7		8/8/8/8		9/8/8/9	10/8/8/10
Rounded stitches, horseshoe	4		4		4		4		5		5		6	6
Stitches, picked up along side of heel flap	11	11	12	12	13	13	14	14	15	15	16	16	17	17
SHORT-ROW HEELS														
Arrangement of heel stitches	7/8/7		8/8/8/		8/10/8		9/10/9		10/10/10		10/12/10		11/12/11	12/12/12
Gusset stitches, hybrid heel	4		4		4		4		5		5		5	6
Number of rows, hybrid heel	8		8		8		8		10		10		10	12
ROUND HEELS ENDING AT THE LOWER HEEL														
Number of stitches, standard heel	4	4	4	4	4	4	5	5	5	5	5	5	6	6
Stitches cast on, standard heel	15	15	16	16	17	17	19	19	20	20	21	21	23	24
Length of foot, waste yarn to toes (in)	3½	4	4	4½	5	5½	6	6½	6½	7	7¾	8	8½	8½
Length of foot, waste yarn to toes (cm)	9	10	10	11½	12½	14	15½	16½	16½	18	19½	20½	21½	21½
Repeat rows after 1st decrease														
on every 4th round		1x	1x	1x	1x	1x	1x	1x	1x	1x	1x	1x	1x	1x
on every 3rd round	3x	2x	2x	2x	2x	2x	2x	2x	2x	2x	2x	2x	2x	2x
on every 2nd round	3x	3x	3x	3x	3x	3x	3x	3x	3x	3x	3x	3x	4x	4x
on every round	1x	1x	1x	1x	1x	1x	1x	1x	2x	2x	1x	2x	1x	2x
Ending heel	6M/Nd						7 M/Nd						8 M/Nd	

LENGTH (IN INCHES) OF THE VARIOUS TOES WITH FINGERING-WEIGHT OR 4-PLY SOCK YARN

1¾ oz./50g, 229 yards/210m, 30 stitches x 42 rows = 4"/10cm

Children's and women's sizes	5/5½	6/7	8/9	9½/10	11/11½	12/13	1/2	3/4	5/6	7/8	9/9½	10/11	12/13	14/15
Men's sizes										5/6	7/8	9/10	11/12	13/14
Continental sizes	20/21	22/23	24/25	26/27	28/29	30/31	32/33	34/35	36/37	38/39	40/41	42/43	44/45	46/47
Total stitches	44	44	48	48	52	52	56	56	60	60	64	64	68	72
Total stitches per needle	11	11	12	12	13	13	14	14	15	15	16	16	17	18
Total length of foot	5¼"	6"	6½"	6¾"	7½"	8"	8½"	9"	9¾"	10"	10¾"	11¼"	11½"	12¼"
Toe band, pulled together	1¼"	1¼"	1¼"	1¼"	1½"	1½"	1¾"	1¾"	2"	2"	2¼"	2¼"	2½"	2½"
Length of foot to start of toes	4¼"	4¾"	5"	5½"	6"	6½"	6¾"	7¼"	7¾"	8"	8½"	9"	9¼"	9½"
Toe band, short			1"	1"	1¼"	1¼"	1¼"	1¼"	1½"	1½"	1½"	1½"	1¾"	1¾"
Length of foot to start of toes			5½"	6"	6¼"	6¾"	7¼"	7¾"	8"	8½"	9"	9½"	9¾"	10½"
Star toes	¾"	¾"	1¼"	1¼"	1¼"	1¼"	1¾"	1¾"	1¾"	1¾"	2½"	2½"	2½"	3¼"
Length of foot to start of toes	4½"	5"	5"	5½"	6¼"	6¾"	6¾"	7¼"	7¾"	8¼"	8"	8¾"	9"	8¾"
Spiral toes	1½"	1½"	1¾"	1¾"	2"	2"	2¼"	2¼"	2¼"	2¼"	2½"	2½"	2¾"	3"
Length of foot to start of toes	3¾"	4¼"	4¾"	5"	5½"	6¼"	6¼"	6¾"	7¼"	7¾"	8"	8¾"	8¾"	9¼"
Propeller toes	1½"	1½"	1¾"	1¾"	2"	2"		2"	2"	2¼"	2¼"	2¼"	2¼"	2½"
Length of foot to start of toes	3¾"	4¼"	4¾"	5"	5½"	6¼"	6¼"	7"	7½"	8"	8¼"	8¾"	9"	9½"
Flower toes	1¼"	1¼"	1¼"	1¼"	1½"	1½"	1½"	1½"	2"	2"	2"	2"	2¼"	2¼
Length of foot to start of toes	4"	4½"	5"	5½"	6"	6¼"	6¾"	7½"	7¾"	8"	8¾"	9¼"	9½"	10"
Short-row heel as toe	1¼"	1¼"	1¼"	1¼"	1½"	1½"	1¾"	1¾"	2"	2"	2"	2"	2¼"	2¼"
Arrangement of stitches	7/8/7	7/8/7	8/8/8	8/8/8	9/8/9	9/8/9	10/8/10	10/8/10	11/8/11	11/8/11	11/10/11	11/10/11	12/10/12	13/10/13
Length of foot to start of toes	4¼"	4¾"	5"	5½"	6"	6½"	6¾"	7¼"	7¾"	8"	8¾"	9¼"	9½"	10"

LENGTH (IN CENTIMETERS) OF THE VARIOUS TOES WITH FINGERING-WEIGHT OR 4-PLY SOCK YARN

1¾ oz./50g, 229 yards/210m, 30 stitches x 42 rows = 4"/10cm

Children's and women's sizes	5/5½	6/7	8/9	9½/10	11/11½	12/13	1/2	3/4	5/6	7/8	9/9½	10/11	12/13	14/15
Men's sizes										5/6	7/8	9/10	11/12	13/14
Continental sizes	20/21	22/23	24/25	26/27	28/29	30/31	32/33	34/35	36/37	38/39	40/41	42/43	44/45	46/47
Total stitches	44	44	48	48	52	52	56	56	60	60	64	64	68	72
Total stitches per needle	11	11	12	12	13	13	14	14	15	15	16	16	17	18
Total length of foot	13½	15	16½	17½	19	20½	21½	23	24½	25½	27	28½	29½	31
Toe band, pulled together	3	3	3½	3½	4	4	4½	4½	5	5	5½	5½	6	6½
Length of foot to start of toes	10½	12	13	14	15	16½	17	18½	19½	20½	21½	23½	23½	24½
Toe band, short			2½	2½	3	3	3	3	4	4	4	4	4½	4½
Length of foot to start of toes			14	15	16	17½	18½	20	20½	21½	23½	24½	25½	26½
Star toes	2	2	3½	3½	3½	3½	4½	4½	4½	4½	6½	6½	6½	8½
Length of foot to start of toes	11½	13	13	14	15½	17	17	18½	20	21	20½	22	23	22½
Spiral toes	4	4	4½	4½	5	5	5½	5½	6	6	6½	6½	7	7½
Length of foot to start of toes	9½	11	12	13	14	15½	16½	18	19	20½	21	22½	23	24
Propeller toes	4	4	4½	4½	5	5	5	5	5½	5½	5½	6	6	6½
Length of foot to start of toes	9½	11	12	13	14	15½	16½	18	19	20½	21	22½	23	24
Flower toes	3½	3½	3½	3½	4	4	4	4	5	5	5	5	5½	5½
Length of foot to start of toes	10	11½	13	14	15½	16½	17½	19	19½	20½	22	23½	24	25½
Short-row heel as toe	3	3	3½	3½	4	4	4½	4½	5	5	5	5	5½	6
Arrangement of stitches	7/8/7	7/8/7	8/8/8	8/8/8	9/8/9	9/8/9	10/8/10	10/8/10	11/8/11	11/8/11	11/10/11	11/10/11	12/10/12	13/10/13
Length of foot to start of toes	10½	12	13	14	15	16½	17	18½	19½	20½	22	23½	24	25

HEEL SIZES WITH DK-WEIGHT OR 6-PLY SOCK YARN

1¾ oz./50g, 136 yards/125m, 22 stitches x 30 rows = 4"/10cm

Children's and women's sizes	5/5½	6/7	8/9	9½/10	11/11½	12/13	1/2	3/4	5/6	7/8	9/9½	10/11	12/13	14/15
Men's sizes										5/6	7/8	9/10	11/12	13/14
Continental sizes	20/21/	22/23	24/25/	26/27	28/29	30/31	32/33	34/35	36/37	38/39	40/41	42/43	44/45	46/47
Stitches (total)	32	32	36	36	40	40	44	44	48	48	52	52	52	56
Stitches per needle	8	8	9	9	10	10	11	11	12	12	13	13	13	14
Heel stitches	16	16	18	18	20	20	22	22	24	24	26	26	26	28
HEEL FLAP STITCHES: HEEL FLAP, HORSESHOE, HEART, AND ROUND HEELS														
Heel height, rows	16	16	18	18	20	20	22	22	24	24	26	26	26	28
Stitches, gusset	5/6/5	6/6/6	6/6/6		6/8/6		7/8/7		8/8/8		8/10/8		8/10/8	9/10/9
Stitches, horseshoe	4/4/4/4		5/4/4/5		6/4/4/6		6/5/5/6		6/6/6/6		7/6/6/7		7/6/6/7	7/7/7/7
Rounded stitches, horseshoe	3	3	3	3	3	3	4	4	4	4	4	4	4	5
Stitches, picked up along side of heel flap	8	8	9	9	10	10	11	11	12	12	13	13	13	14
SHORT-ROW HEELS														
Arrangement of heel stitches	5/6/5	5/6/5	6/6/6	6/6/6	6/8/6	6/8/6	7/8/7	7/8/7	8/8/8	8/8/8	8/10/8	8/10/8	8/10/8	9/18/9
Gusset stitches, hybrid heel	3	3	3	3	3	3	4	4	4	4	4	4	4	5
Number of rows, hybrid heel	6	6	6	6	6	6	8	8	8	8	8	8	8	10
ROUND HEELS ENDING AT THE LOWER HEEL														
Number of stitches, standard heel	3	3	3	3	3	3	4	4	4	4	4	4	4	5
Stitches cast on, standard heel	11	11	12	12	13	13	15	15	16	16	17	17	17	18
Length of foot, waste yarn to toes (in)	3½	4	4	4½	5	5½	6	6½	6½	7	7¾	8	8½	8½
Length of foot, waste yarn to toes (cm)	9	10	10	11½	12½	14	15½	16½	16½	18	19½	20½	21½	21½
Repeat rows after 1st decrease														
on every 4th round														2x
on every 3rd round					1x	1x	1x	1x	1x	1x	2x	2x	1x	1x
on every 2nd round	3x	3x	3x	3x	3x	3x	3x	3x	3x	3x	3x	3x	3x	3x
on every round	1x	1x	2x	2x	2x	2x	2x	2x	3x	3x	3x	3x	2x	
Ending heel	3M/Nd						4 M/Nd							5 M/Nd

123

LENGTH (IN INCHES) OF THE VARIOUS TOES WITH DK-WEIGHT OR 6-PLY SOCK YARN

1¾ oz./50g, 136 yards/125m, 22 stitches x 30 rows = 4"/10cm

Children's and women's sizes	5/5½	6/7	8/9	9½/10	11/11½	12/13	1/2	3/4	5/6	7/8	9/9½	10/11	12/13	14/15
Men's sizes										5/6	7/8	9/10	11/12	13/14
Continental sizes	20/21	22/23	24/25	26/27	28/29	30/31	32/33	34/35	36/37	38/39	40/41	42/43	44/45	46/47
Total stitches	32	32	36	36	40	40	44	44	48	48	52	52	52	56
Total stitches per needle	8	8	9	9	10	10	11	11	12	12	13	13	13	14
Total length of foot	5¼"	6"	6½"	6¾"	7½"	8"	8½"	9"	9¾"	10"	10¾"	11¼"	11½"	12¼"
Toe band, pulled together	1¼"	1¼"	1¼"	1¼"	1½"	1½"	1¾"	1¾"	2"	2"	2¼"	2¼"	2¼"	2½"
Length of foot to start of toes	4¼"	4¾"	5"	5½"	6"	6½"	6¾"	7¼"	7¾"	8"	8½"	9"	9½"	9¾"
Toe band, short			1"	1"	1¼"	1¼"	1¼"	1¼"	1½"	1½"	2"	2"	2"	2¼"
Length of foot to start of toes			5½"	6"	6¼'	6¾"	7"	7¾"	8"	8½"	8¾"	9¼"	9½"	10"
Star toes	¾"	¾"	¾"	¾"	1¼"	1¼"	1¼"	1¼"	1¾"	1¾"	1¾"	1¾"	1¾"	2½"
Length of foot to start of toes	4½"	5"	5¾"	6"	6¼"	6¾"	7¼"	8"	8"	8¼"	8¾"	9½"	9¾"	10"
Spiral toes	1¼"	1¼"	1½"	1½"	1¾"	1¾"	2¼"	2¼"	2¼"	2¼"	2½"	2½"	2½"	3¼"
Length of foot to start of toes	1¼"	1¼"	1½"	1½"	1¾"	1¾"	2"	2"	2¼"	2¼"	2¼"	2¼"	2¼"	2½"
Propeller toes	1¼"	1¼"	1½"	1½"	1¾"	1¾"	2"	2"	2¼"	2¼"	2¼"	2¼"	2¼"	2½"
Length of foot to start of toes	4"	4½"	5"	5¼"	5¾"	6¼"	6½"	7"	7¼"	7¾"	8¼"	8¾"	9¼"	9½"
Flower toes	1"	1"	1½"	1½"	1½"	1½"	1¾"	1¾"	1¾"	1¾"	2¼"	2¼"	2¼"	2¼"
Length of foot to start of toes	4¼"	5"	5"	5½"	6"	6¾"	6¾"	7¼"	7¾"	8¼"	8½"	9"	9½"	10"
Short-row heel as toe	1¼"	1¼"	1¼"	1¼"	1¼"	1¼"	1½"	1½"	1½"	1½"	2¼"	2¼"	2¼"	2¼"
Arrangement of stitches	5/6/5	5/6/5	6/6/6	6/6/6	6/8/6	6/8/6	7/8/7	7/8/7	8/8/8	8/8/8	9/9/9	9/9/9	9/9/9	9/10/9
Length of foot to start of toes	4"	4¾"	5"	5½"	6"	6¾"	6¾"	7½"	8"	8½"	8½"	9"	9½"	10"

LENGTH (IN CENTIMETERS) OF THE VARIOUS TOES WITH DK-WEIGHT OR 6-PLY SOCK YARN

1¾ oz./50g, 136 yards/125m, 22 stitches x 30 rows = 4"/10cm

Children's and women's sizes	5/5½	6/7	8/9	9½/10	11/11½	12/13	1/2	3/4	5/6	7/8	9/9½	10/11	12/13	14/15
Men's sizes										5/6	7/8	9/10	11/12	13/14
Continental sizes	20/21	22/23	24/25	26/27	28/29	30/31	32/33	34/35	36/37	38/39	40/41	42/43	44/45	46/47
Total stitches	32	32	36	36	40	40	44	44	48	48	52	52	52	56
Total stitches per needle	8	8	9	9	10	10	11	11	12	12	13	13	13	14
Total length of foot	13½	15½	16½	17½	19	20½	21½	23	24½	25½	27	28½	29½	31
Toe band, pulled together	3	3	3½	3½	4	4	4½	4½	5	5	5½	5½	5½	6½
Length of foot to start of toes	10½	12	13	14	15	16½	17	18½	19½	20½	21½	23	24	24½
Toe band, short			2½	2½	3	3	3½	3½	4	4	5	5	5	5½
Length of foot to start of toes			14	15	16	17½	18	19½	20½	21½	22	23½	24½	25½
Star toes	2	2	2	2	3	3	3	3	4½	4½	4½	4½	4½	6½
Length of foot to start of toes	11½	13	14½	15½	16	17½	18½	20½	20½	21	22½	24	25	25½
Spiral toes	3½	3½	4	4	4½	4½	5½	5½	6	6	6½	6½	6½	8½
Length of foot to start of toes	3½	3½	4	4	4½	4½	5	5	5½	5½	6	6	6	6½
Propeller toes	3½	3½	4	4	4½	4½	5	5	5½	5½	6	6	6	6½
Length of foot to start of toes	10½	11½	12½	13½	14½	16	16½	18	19	20	21	22½	23½	24
Flower toes	2½	2½	3½	3½	3½	3/12	4½	4½	4½	4½	5½	5½	5½	5½
Length of foot to start of toes	11	12½	13	14	15½	17	17	18½	20	21	21½	23	24	25½
Short-row heel as toe	3	3	3½	3½	3½	3½	4	4	4	4	5½	5½	5½	5½
Arrangement of stitches	5/6/5	5/6/5	6/6/6	6/6/6	6/8/6	6/8/6	7/8/7	7/8/7	8/8/8	8/8/8	9/9/9	9/9/9	9/9/9	9/10/9
Length of foot to start of toes	10½	12	13	14	15½	17	17½	19	20½	21½	21½	23	24	25½

The patterns in this book feature Regia Yarns. We urge you to explore the inspiring array of sock yarns that are available to knitters by visiting the manufacturers' sites listed here.

Yarn suppliers

BLUE MOON FIBER ARTS
www.bluemoonfiberarts.com
866-802-9687

CHERRY TREE HILL
www.cherryyarn.com
802-525-3311

CLAUDIA HAND PAINTED YARNS
www.claudiaco.com
540-433-1140

COLINETTE
www.colinette.com
01938 810128

DREAM IN COLOR
www.dreamincoloryarn.com

FIESTA YARNS
www.fiestayarns.com
505-892-5008

FLEECE ARTIST
www.fleeceartist.com
902-462-0800

J. KNITS
www.j-knits.com
888-395-8261

LISA SOUZA KNITWEAR AND DYEWORKS
www.lisaknit.com
530-647-1183

LORNA'S LACES
www.lornaslaces.net
773-935-3803

LOUET
www.louet.com
613-925-1405

MALABRIGO YARN
www.magabrigo.com
786-866-6187

OPAL
www.opalsockyarn.com
877-603-6725

PAGEWOOD FARM
www.pagewoodfarm.com
310-831-6810

SHIBUI KNITS
www.shibuiknits.com
971-678-1721

Online help

www.persistentillusion.com
www.socknitters.com

Magazines

Creative Knitting
www.creativeknittingmagazine.com

Interweave Knits
www.interweaveknits.com

Knit 'N Style
www.knitnstyle.com

Knitter's
www.knittersmagazine.com

Knitter's Review
www.knittersreview.com

Knitty
www.knitty.com

Verena Knitting
www.verenaknitting.com

Vogue Knitting
www.vogueknitting.com

Suggested Reading

Hemingway, Karen. *Super Stitches Knitting: Knitting Essentials Plus a Dictionary of More Than 300 Stitch Patterns.* New York: Watson-Guptill Publications, 2007.

Johnson, Wendy D. *Socks from the Toe Up: Essential Techniques and Patterns from Wendy Knits.* New York: Potter Craft, 2009.

Queen, Nancy and O'Connell, Mary Ellen. *The Chicks with Sticks Guide to Knitting: Learn to Knit with More Than 30 Cool, Easy Patterns.* New York: Watson-Guptill Publications, 2008.

Basics and tips, 11–17
    about: overview of, 11
    avoiding holes, 13
    correct needle size, 12
    design basics, 17
    grafting (Kitchener stitch), 15
    joining yarn (Russian way), 16
    knit stitches, 14
    knitting gauge swatch, 12
    numbering double-pointed needles, 12
    starting self-patterning yarns, 13
    transporting double-pointed needles, 16
    unwinding yarn, 12
    weaving in yarn tails, 16
Binding off, 90–92
Care instructions, 6
Casting on, 19–27
    figure eight, 82
    to four needles, 19
    invisible method, 27, 85, 86–87
    loop method, 27, 83
    number of stitches for, 20
    to one needle, 19
    slip knot for, 20
    thumb methods, 21–22
    tubular (Italian) methods, 23–25, 30
    two-needle method, 26
Circular needles, 9
    knitting socks with one (flat, back and
        forth), 97
    knitting socks with one (in round), 95–96
    knitting socks with two, 93–95
Classic design with heel flap, 17
Components of socks, illustrated, 11
Cuffs, 29–35
    determining height of, 29
    double, 32–33
    frilly, 33
    garter, 31
    illustrated, 11
    leg and, 35
    ribbed, 29–30
    rolled, 34
Design basics, 17
Diagonal seam heel for toes, 77–78
Diagonal seam heels. *See* Heels with
    diagonal seams
Diagonal toe shaping, 85
Double-beaded selvage, 41
Double-decrease band, 65, 69, 82
Double-pointed needles, 7–8, 12, 16
Double stitches
    lesson on working, 53
    reinforced, short-row heel with, 56
    short-row heel with, 53–54
Elastic thumb cast-on method, 22
Figure eight cast-on, 82
Fold edging, 33
Foundation row, illustrated, 11. *See also*
    Casting on
Gauge swatches, 12
Grafting (Kitchener stitch), 15
Gussets
    horseshoe, 45–46, 47
    illustrated, 11
    with increases and decreases, 60–61, 62
    picking up stitches and, 44, 47, 51, 62
Heel flap, illustrated, 11. *See also* **Heels
    with heel flaps**
Heels
    avoiding holes, 39, 41
    boomerang, 17
    fitting, 37–38

    increasing through horizontal strand, 39
    keeping track of needles, 38
    leaving stitches on needles 2 and 3, 38
    round, joined at foot, 64–69
    size charts, 120, 123
    for toe-up socks, 87–89
    types of, 39. *See also* specific types
    working, tips, 38–39
Heels with diagonal seams, 52–63
    gusset with increases and decreases,
        60–61, 62
    hybrid heel, 61–62
    mock short-row heel, 63
    other uses for, 52
    short-row heel, 53–55
    short-row heel with reinforced double
        stitches, 56
    short-row heel with round shaping, 57
    short rows and extended short rows, 52
    working double stitches, 53–54, 56
    wrap stitch heel, 58–60
Heels with heel flaps, 17, 40–51
    double-beaded selvage, 41
    picking up new stitches along double-
        beaded selvage, 41
    reinforcing, 42, 47
    round heel, 49–51
    shapes of heel, 40
    tips on working, 41–42
    turning heart-shaped over 2 panels, 48–49
    turning horseshoe over 4 panels, 45–47
    turning over 3 panels, 43–45
Holes, avoiding, 13, 39, 41, 50, 52
Horseshoe leg, 47
Interwoven reinforcement, 42
Italian bind-off, 91–92
Joining yarn, 16
Kitchener stitch (grafting), 15
Knit stitches, 14
Knitwise
    avoiding holes, 13
    defined, 13
    right- and left-slanting decreases, 14
Leg
    illustrated, 11
    working, 35
Mock heel, for toe-up socks, 84
Needles
    circular, 9, 93–97
    composition of, 7–8
    double-pointed, 7–8, 12, 16
    numbering, 12
    sizes, 5, 12, 119
    transporting, 16
Netting, reinforced, 42, 89
Patterns
    about: making rows into rounds, 118;
        notation of, 116; other considerations,
        118–119; skill levels/icons, 98;
        transferring to charts, 117
    Anatomical Socks, 108
    Baby's Socks, 99
    Basket Weave Socks, 114–115
    Chevron Socks, 102
    Entirely Natural, 101
    Folklore Socks, 113
    Garter Waves, 100
    Mosaic Pattern, 112
    For Mother and Daughter, 105–106
    Ribs and Cables, 109
    Socks for Shopping, 111
    Sport Socks, 110
    A Timeless Classic, 104

    Wavy Stripes, 107
    For the Well-Respected Man, 103
Picot edging, 33
Purlwise, defined, 13
**Reinforced (double) thumb cast-on method,
    22**
Reinforcing heels, 42, 47
Ribs, reinforced, 42, 89
Rounded horseshoe shape, 46
Round heels joined at the foot, 64–69
    "afterthought" heel with waste yarn, 69
    closing heel, 64–65
    peasant heel, 67–69
    plain heel, 66–67
    tips on working, 64–65
Round shaping, short-row heel with, 57
Rows, making into rounds, 118
Scalloped edging, 33
Self-patterning yarns, 13
Short rows and extended short rows, 52
Supplies, 5–9
Toes, 71–79
    anatomically shaped, 73
    decreases, illustrated, 11
    diagonal seam heel for, 77–78
    flower, 76
    illustrated, 11
    length charts, 121–122, 124–125
    paired-decrease, 71–72
    propeller, 78–79
    spiral, 75
    star, 73–74, 82
    tips for length of foot and, 79
Toe-up socks
    about: overview of, 81
    casting on, 82–83
    diagonal toe shaping, 85
    finishes for, 90–92
    heels for, 87–89
    horizontal toe bands, 86
    mock heel, 84
    toes, 82–87
    toe shaping using invisible cast-on, 86–87
Turning heels
    heart-shaped heel over 2 panels, 48–49
    horseshoe heel over 4 panels, 45–47
    illustrated, 11
    over 3 panels, 43–45
    round heel, 49–51
Twisted garter cuff, 31
Twisted ribbed cuffs, 29, 30
Weaving in yarn tails, 16
Wrap stitches, lesson on working, 58
Yarns
    Baby-weight, 5, 119
    blends, 6
    care instructions, 6
    DK-weight, 5, 104, 119
    fiber and plies, 5
    fingering-weight, 5, 99, 100–103, 105,
        107–114, 119
    joining, Russian way, 16
    label icons, 6
    lace-weight, 5, 119
    needle sizes for, 5, 12, 119
    number of stitches to cast on.
        See Casting on
    self-patterning, starting with, 13
    sport-weight, 5, 119
    suppliers, 126
    types, uses, specifications, 5, 118
    unwinding from inside of ball/skein, 12

EVA JOSTES and **STEPHANIE VAN DER LINDEN** are experienced knitters and teachers of sock-knitting techniques. They have done extensive research on the best sock-knitting materials, colors, and fit, and are co-authors of several books on the subject. Both Ewa's and Stephanie's work can be seen on Ravelry, and Stephanie is a contributor to the Internet knitting magazine www.twistcollective.com. They both live in Germany.

ACKNOWLEDGMENTS

We would like to thank Coats, Coats GmbH, Kenzingen, Germany, (www.coatsgmbh.de) and Prym Consumer Europe, Stolberg, Germany (www.prym-consumer.com) for their support in producing this book.

Translation copyright © 2010 by Watson-Guptill Publications, an imprint of the Crown Publishing Group, a division of Random House, Inc.

All rights reserved.

Published in the United States by Watson-Guptill Publications, an imprint of the Crown Publishing Group, a division of Random House, Inc., New York.

www.crownpublishing.com
www.watsonguptill.com

WATSON-GUPTILL is a registered trademark and the WG and Horse designs are trademarks of Random House, Inc.

Originally published in hardcover in Germany as Der geniale Socken-Workshop by frechverlag GmbH, Stuttgart, Germany (www.frech.de), in 2007.

Copyright © 2007 by frechverlag GmbH. This edition is published in arrangement with Claudia Böhme Rights & Literary Agency, Hanover, Germany (www.agency-boehme.com).

This work also contains material from Socken stricken by Tanja Steinbach, originally published in Germany by frechverlag GmbH, Stuttgart, Germany (www.frech.de), in 2006.

Copyright © 2006 by frechverlag GmbH.

Library of Congress Cataloging-in-Publication Data

ISBN 978-0-8230-8553-8

Printed in China

Concept, product management, and lector: Giovanna Lo Presti

Layout: Petra Theilfarth

Photos: frechverlag GmbH, 70499 Stuttgart; Fotostudio Ullrich & Co., Renningen

10 9 8 7 6 5 4 3 2 1

First American Edition